Scholarly Publishing

A Short Guide

Jo VanEvery, PhD

Scholarly Publishing

Short Guides, vol 3

Copyright © 2019 Jo VanEvery

All rights reserved.

ISBN: 978-1-912040-68-1 (pb) 978-1-912040-67-4 (e-book)

No part of this publication may be reproduced, stored in a retrieval system, or transmitted in any form or by any means, electronic, mechanical, photocopying, recording, or otherwise, without the prior written permission of the copyright owner.

This book is sold subject to the condition that it shall not, by way of trade or otherwise, be lent, resold, hired out, or otherwise circulated without the publisher's prior consent in any form of binding or cover other than that in which it is published and without a similar condition including this condition being imposed on the subsequent purchaser. Under no circumstances may any part of this book be photocopied for resale.

Cover Design: Amy Crook

Jo Van Every

Table of Contents

About the Short Guides Series 1

About This Guide 4

What is Publishing and Why Do It? 7

Audience, Form, Outlet 19

Books 35

Peer-Reviewed Journals 67

Publishing Work in Progress 88

Improving Discoverability 106

Notes and Further Reading 123

Acknowledgements 140

About the Author 143

About the Short Guides Series

My journey to becoming an academic career guide began in 2005, though I didn't call it that at the time. In the early years, my work focused on supporting Canadian social science and humanities academics with grant applications. Drawing on my experience as a programme officer and policy analyst at the Social Sciences and Humanities Research Council of Canada, and my own eight-year academic career as a sociologist in the UK, I focused on helping academics understand how funding competitions worked, improving their project descriptions, and advising them on their applications.

Two issues came up repeatedly. The first was the quantity and quality of previous publications. Many of my clients expressed frustration with the publication record required to be competitive, especially if they worked in institutions with heavier teaching loads. The second, related issue was the concept of "impact on the advancement of knowledge". Many academics were confused about why some scholarly publications were more highly valued than others, and how such publications related to the increasingly pressing demand to reach audiences beyond the academy. This confusion had consequences for their ability to frame their research in relation to its likely impact on the advancement of knowledge, as well as their confidence in the importance of the questions they most wanted to research.

The impossibility of addressing these difficulties on a short-term basis (difficulties that, after all, affect much more than just the ability to secure funding) was frustrating for everyone. In 2009, I started shifting my focus to take a longer-term view, creating a website (JoVanEvery.ca) and starting to blog. In 2011, I started A Meeting With Your Writing, a synchronous virtual writing group, as a way of providing practical support to academics who were struggling to protect their writing time due to the pressures of all their other responsibilities. I gradually built a coaching practice that wasn't focused directly on grant applications, sharing what I was learning through my blog.

By 2015, I had over 400 blog posts, most of them still relevant but a bit difficult to find in the archive. The *Short Guides* series organizes, summarizes, and builds on those blog posts to create practical resources based on what I've learned over the years. An important underlying principle of the *Short Guides* is that there are many different ways to do most things. You have particular values and goals. Your brain and body work in particular ways. You work in a specific kind of institution with its own values and goals. Things that used to work well for you stop working. Your priorities change over time. You need to make decisions — and maybe experiment with new strategies — in light of how all these things come together, right now, for you.

Each *Short Guide* focuses on one area of your academic life, providing advice in a format you can apply to your own specific circumstances. I've started with topics related to scholarly writing. They are short, so you can spend more time writing and less time reading about writing or time management. They are practical, suggesting strategies you can try right now. I expect you will read each *Short Guide* through from beginning to end when you first acquire it. However, they are really intended to be kept close by, so you can refer to the section that addresses your current frustration as and when needed. Coffee rings have been pre-applied, so don't feel guilty about using a *Short Guide* as a coaster.

Enjoy your writing!

Other *Short Guides*

The Scholarly Writing Process: A Short Guide (2016)
ISBN 978-1-912040-64-3 (pb) 978-1-912040-72-8 (e-book)

Finding Time For Your Scholarly Writing: A Short Guide (2018)
ISBN 978-1-912040-70-4 (pb) 978-1-912040-69-8 (e-book)

About This Guide

In *Scholarly Publishing*, I focus on the big picture of publishing for scholarly audiences and the questions you need to ask yourself to make good decisions at every stage of your project. There is a lot of information and advice out there, much of it in the form of rules or exhortations. In *Scholarly Publishing*, I outline the principles so you can figure out the right course of action for your particular situation. I expect you to seek out more detailed information about specific publishing options and the culture and expectations of your discipline and institution.

Scholarly Publishing is a companion volume to *The Scholarly Writing Process*. There is a point in the process where you shift from writing to articulate your thoughts to writing to produce a product that will communicate those thoughts to a specific audience. I introduced the topic of specifying your audience and prioritizing a particular product in *The Scholarly Writing Process*. I expand on it in this *Short Guide* and provide more information to help you make those decisions.

In addition to publishing for scholarly audiences, you may communicate your scholarly work with people who are not scholars. Depending where you are located, this may be called "wider impact", "knowledge mobilization", "knowledge transfer", "knowledge translation", or "public outreach". The strategies required to reach these audiences are significantly different, warranting separate attention. These audiences are introduced briefly in this volume to help you situate your scholarly publishing in relation to other ways of publishing your research.

I suggest reading through the guide once to get a sense of the general principles and how they apply to specific types of publications. You can use the principles to help you make an overall publishing plan. You can then return to specific sections when you are considering specific types of outputs from your work. This guide will also be helpful when you are deciding what to do next with a conference paper or series of blog posts, when a manuscript has been rejected from a journal, or if you are not going to make the deadline for a special issue or edited book. There are questions at the end of each chapter to help you relate the advice to your particular situation. I encourage you to actually write out your answers to the questions. You are a writer. Writing is how you process your thoughts.

Publishing is difficult, even for experienced writers. It's hard to feel positive *in general* about what are objectively scary things like putting your work out there. Thinking about a *specific* piece can help focus on specific things that will mitigate those fears and help move it forward. I don't want to minimise the genuine fear/discomfort associated with publishing. I want to help you figure out how to move forward despite that. The discomfort might always be there until you figure out specific things about a particular paper.

My aim in publishing *Scholarly Publishing* is to help you get your ideas out to the audience that needs to hear them, get feedback on your writing in progress, keep your writing projects moving forward, and ensure your writing process results in publications. Keep this guide close by and refer to it whenever you need to.

Enjoy your writing!

Jo VanEvery
High Peak, UK

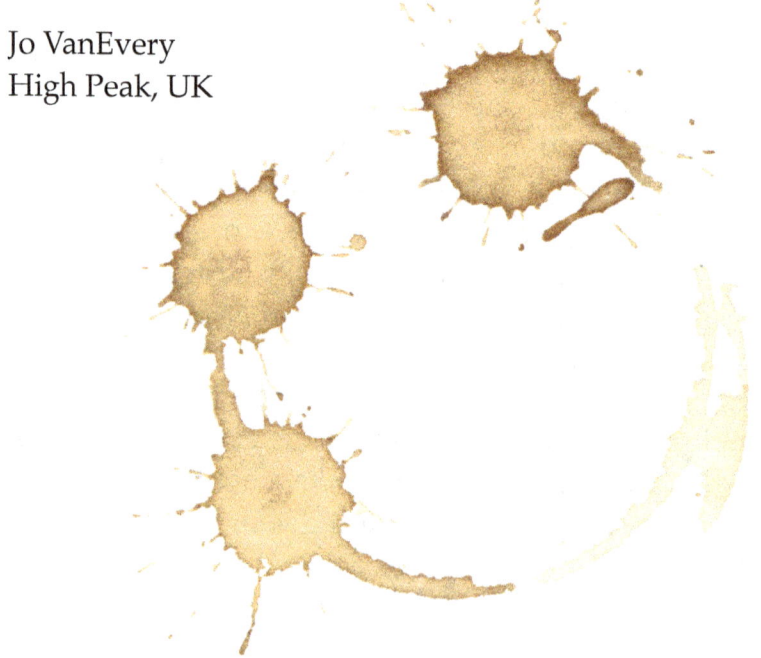

What is Publishing and Why Do It?

The term "publishing" derives from the Latin *publicare*—to make public. The pressure to publish comes, in part, from your desire to communicate. You do this work because you are excited about your research, your findings, and your ideas. Once you get to the point in the writing process where you have a reasonably coherent way of expressing things, you want to share your work. There are people who need to know this.

> Think of publishing in the broadest sense of the word. A transfer from brain to brain, via some sort of tool. (Margaret Atwood)

There are myriad means of doing so. (Atwood starts her list with yelling.)

The primary purpose of academic and scholarly publishing is to communicate with other scholars. When you publish, you are making a contribution to scholarly knowledge. When you publish in a scholarly outlet, you are not setting out a definitive, incontestable, truth. You aren't trying to win an argument. You are contributing to an ongoing conversation. You are adding one piece that brings us closer to truth. You are inspiring other people to work on this more, to extend what you've done, or to demonstrate that their approach to this question is better.

Contributing to the scholarly conversation is daunting, especially if you are relatively new to it. Thinking about scholarly publishing may trigger insecurity about your ideas, your ability to communicate them well, or whether anyone is even interested in communicating with you about them. You may find that the painfully slow processes of scholarly publishing are out of sync with your enthusiasm for your work. You may fear that, by the time you get your work out there, it will no longer be relevant. Those fears and insecurities are strong indications of your intrinsic desire to publish.

There is also external pressure to publish, due to the role publishing plays in your career and in validating your identity and status as a scholar. As Aileen Fyfe and colleagues point out in their introduction to *Untangling Academic Publishing*:

> Academic publishing is not simply an industry adapting to technological innovation. It is a system that underpins claims to new scholarly knowledge, and it is a major influence on the professional standing of the 200,000 academic researchers working in UK universities and their peers worldwide. Academic publishing is central to systems for recognising prestige, and is widely used as a form of symbolic capital by the scholarly community and its institutions.

Unfortunately, this validation narrative has become the dominant narrative frame for discussing scholarly publishing: *Will this count? How will this count? Am I wasting my time writing this if it won't count?* The work itself can seem incidental to the achievement of having a publication in a high-ranking journal.

When you come to actually write, the validation narrative is often what gets you stuck. The reason your paper doesn't seem good enough to send off is not because you don't have something to say but because you think of publishing as validating your worth, rather than communicating your knowledge. The degree of stuck is exacerbated if you are sceptical of the validation process itself. Focusing on the communicative role of publishing—what you want to say, and to whom—can be a powerful road out of the stuck. It puts the focus on the work itself and the conversation you will engage in.

An important part of academic freedom is the ability to prioritize which audiences you will write for and which scholarly conversations you will engage in. That freedom is somewhat constrained, so your stage of career and your career goals will influence your priorities. This guide will help you figure out what your options are, so you can balance your *communicative* goals with the needs of whichever validation processes are important for you at this stage of your career.

How communicative goals relate to the validation process

By focusing on the communicative role of publishing, I do not want to suggest that the role your publications play in various evaluation and validation processes is unimportant. Rather, I am asking you to trust that those processes are based on values you share (to some extent) with whoever is evaluating your work. One barrier to that trust is the fact that the values underpinning validation processes have become obscured, even to those doing the evaluation. The indicators used to evaluate scholarship—citations, reputation of the press or journal, etc.—have become disconnected from the thing they are meant to indicate. The primary reasons you communicate your research are to *make a contribution to the advancement of knowledge* and (ideally) *have a significant impact on the advancement of knowledge*.

Whether they use the term "contribution," "impact," or "significance," validation processes were designed to evaluate the likelihood that your work will make a difference to those who engage with it. These are the values you share with the institutions that evaluate your publications. The quality of your work is important, but only insofar as you don't want poor-quality work to influence either scholarly or public debates. It is not enough to do good-quality scholarly work; you must also communicate your knowledge.

By publishing in scholarly outlets, you are making your knowledge available to a community of scholars. Some of those scholars will read your article, perhaps multiple times. They may engage with your ideas and evidence in their own scholarly work. Depending on how directly and strongly your work influences theirs, they will cite your work when they publish their own contributions to this scholarly conversation, just as you cite those who have influenced your work. Some of those who read your work will recommend it to others, individually or in more formal ways, whether or not it is directly relevant to their own work at the time of reading. They may include it in the syllabus for a course they are teaching. They may recommend it to students or postdoctoral researchers they are supervising. They may recommend it to colleagues to whom it may be more relevant. They may publish a review. They may talk about it on social media.

Your communication goals and your validation goals intersect. This takes place at the point where your personal priorities intersect with the priorities of whichever institution evaluates your publication record. Determine the types of impact you value most. You can then decide on your publishing priorities, taking into account the values and priorities of those who will evaluate your output. If specific evaluation processes figure prominently in your career planning, you must carefully consider how different options for publishing your scholarly work will be seen in those processes.

Although different validation processes share many features, there is some variability. Being evaluated for a funding competition is different from being evaluated for hiring or promotion, for example. Hiring and promotion processes vary by institution and take into account the mission and values of the institution. Institutional missions change over time, which can mean that newer hires are evaluated against different criteria than those their senior colleagues were evaluated against at a similar stage of career. Transparency about evaluation criteria, journal rankings, and number of publications required varies considerably, and may be hard to pin down due to the competitive nature of some processes (e.g. funding competitions). Competition can ratchet up de facto requirements far beyond those stated in policy.

Understanding how you will be evaluated in specific processes is something you need to discuss with knowledgeable mentors in your own discipline and institution. Speaking to mentors who have served on evaluation committees is particularly valuable. Be aware that fear-based rumours and speculation circulate among those whose only knowledge of the processes comes from being evaluated. As you progress in your career, opportunities to participate in evaluation committees will improve your understanding of these processes, helping you navigate them better and provide better mentorship to colleagues and students.

It can be difficult to judge how well your communicative goals align with the values likely to inform the specific process in which your work will be evaluated, especially when there is a lot of talk about the importance of things like "interdisciplinarity" and "communicating with wider audiences" that may not actually be reflected in evaluation committees' decisions. In general, your scholarly peers care about contributions to the discipline as a foundation for those other forms of scholarly communication. If the audience you most care about communicating with is not the audience those evaluating your body of work most care about, it doesn't mean you are not doing good work; it means your values are not aligned. If you are in this situation, I encourage you to find mentors in your field who are communicating with the kinds of audiences you value, and get their advice on how that work is valued in practice and how to navigate this terrain. There are points in your career where you may need to prioritize work that your colleagues value in order to secure the job that enables you to do more of the other work you value.

Indicators of impact on the advancement of knowledge

Even with the guidance of mentors, you still need to make your own decisions about how much you want to compromise and how to apply general advice to a specific situation. To assist you in weighing up the different considerations, it may be helpful to further specify the different ways you make an impact on the advancement of knowledge. Drawing on research about the ways in which non-academic audiences (policy makers, practitioners, and so on) use research, and expanding the conceptual framework to encompass impacts on scholarly audiences, we can distinguish three types of research impact.

Instrumental impact is the easiest to measure, because the research (or even a particular publication) has a direct effect on how someone does their work. In scholarly contexts, this includes someone else using your theoretical or methodological framework in their own work, referring directly to your work when making their argument, etc. In the contexts of policy or practice, this kind of impact would be a policy or practice change made as a direct result of your research. The direct connection between your published work and the work impacted requires formal acknowledgement of some kind. While there is a lot of debate about whether citations are an accurate measure of the quality of scholarly work, there is no doubt that impact of this type will require a citation. Even if someone cites your work because they disagree with it, the citation indicates that your work was one important spark that got their writing process started. It is worth noting that research on government use of research suggests that instrumental impact is relatively rare in the policy context. When you consider your own practices in terms of reading and citation it seems safe to assume that, in the scholarly context, citations are the visible part of a larger iceberg.

Conceptual impact occurs when the research changes how others think about something in a more general way. This type is by far the most common type of non-academic use of scholarly research. While conceptual impact may lead indirectly to measurable outcomes, like a new policy or practice, the connection between the outcome and the research is less direct and may not be acknowledged directly. I suspect this is also very common in scholarly impact. Scholarly work is influenced by the accretion of a wide body of knowledge over a long period. Students' struggles with over-citation as a hedge against under-citation (and possible plagiarism) can be seen as a glimpse of the process by which all scholars have learned which influences are worthy of direct citation and which may be left uncited, or cited in a more general way. While citations indicate some of this kind of impact, it may be difficult or impossible to measure conceptual impact accurately. You may need to trust that you are contributing to the advancement of knowledge in this general way.

Symbolic impact is the most troubling type, because it throws into question the validity and reliability of measures of (instrumental) impact and significance. The post-hoc justification of a government policy, where policy makers reference research that supports a particular policy direction, is one obvious example. In scholarly contexts, citations added to a publication to endear yourself to the editor of a particular journal or to highlight the influence of someone with whom you are trying to build a research relationship might be considered symbolic impact. Although this type of attribution may involve an erroneous or partial use of the cited research, more commonly it is appropriate but selective citation with a symbolic purpose. This kind of symbolic citation (or research use) cannot be summarily dismissed, but it makes it very difficult to determine the significance of the work cited.

Citations are part of the mix of indicators used to evaluate your publication record because they do indicate impact—however imperfectly. But they are not the only indicator used. In addition to the aforementioned points, there is a significant time delay between your own publication and the publication of work citing your publication. This is where quantitative measures like journal impact factors and more subjective understandings of the reputation, readership, and influence of particular journals and presses come in. In many situations, you are being evaluated on your probable future impact on the advancement of knowledge. No one has reliable methods of predicting the future.

The system is not perfect—but you still need to submit to this system. There are points where you will make decisions based on the most effective way of doing well in the system as it manifests in your specific situation. There are times when you need to follow your own path. My hope is that the framework outlined in this chapter and the information about specific options provided in the following chapters will give you a better sense of the context in which you are making those decisions so you can make them confidently.

Some questions to consider

What has prompted you to consider publishing right now?

Has someone suggested it to you? If so, what was their reasoning? (Notice both communication and validation reasons.)

What was your initial reaction to the statement "The primary purpose of academic and scholarly publishing is to communicate with other scholars" and how did that change once you'd read more about the ways communication is embedded in validation processes?

Is there any particular way of sharing your work that makes you feel anxious or panicky?

Can you identify what contributes to your anxiety about this medium?

What stories are you telling yourself about this way of sharing your work?

Are your stories true? Partially true? Are you extrapolating unreasonably?

What would make you feel more comfortable about sharing your work?

Thinking of the particular project that you are under pressure (internal or external) to publish right now:

What difference do you hope it will make? To whom?

What might direct, instrumental impact look like?

What might conceptual impact look like?

Does thinking about impact and significance in this way change how you think about publishing this piece? How?

Is there any particular way of sharing your work that feels reasonably comfortable?

Can you identify what contributes to your comfort with this medium?

Audience, Form, Outlet

A Twitter follower alerted me to this description of publishing as communication by Kenneth Burke (published in 1941):

> Imagine that you enter a parlor. You come late. When you arrive, others have long preceded you, and they are engaged in a heated discussion, a discussion too heated for them to pause and tell you exactly what it is about. In fact, the discussion had already begun long before any of them got there, so that no one present is qualified to retrace for you all the steps that had gone before. You listen for a while, until you decide that you have caught the tenor of the argument; then you put in your oar. Someone answers; you answer him; another comes to your defense; another aligns himself against you, to either the embarrassment or gratification of your opponent, depending upon the quality of your ally's assistance. However, the discussion is interminable. The hour grows late, you must depart. And you do depart, with the discussion still vigorously in progress.

The first step in deciding how and where you will publish your writing is deciding which conversation(s) you want to contribute to. Then you can determine who else is involved in those conversations and where they are happening. This may seem odd. These may be people you could never imagine actually standing in a room with. Some of these people might be dead. The benefit of publishing an article or book is that it is a written contribution to an asynchronous conversation. It allows you to have a conversation that you might not otherwise be able to have. In this *Short Guide*, I am focusing specifically on publishing to engage in scholarly conversations, but the principles apply to all types of publication.

Your scholarly work creates knowledge relevant to several scholarly conversations. Different kinds of scholars are engaged in different kinds of conversations and are interested in different aspects of your work. You may also identify conversations that include practitioners, policy makers, or other non-academic interlocutors, with or without scholarly participants. You may have something to contribute to several conversations, but the effectiveness of your contribution depends on communicating in a way that engages with the specific conversation to which you are contributing.

Your publications are the public face of your research and scholarship. Even when you have moved beyond the early curiosity phase and identified a relatively bounded set of questions, evidence, and arguments, you will publish multiple products. You will publish some kind of work in progress—conference paper, blog post, working paper—where getting feedback before publishing something more substantial and formal, like a journal article, is an explicit goal. You may have things to contribute to specific sub-disciplinary conversations and more general conversations within your discipline. You will publish in different journals (or different formats) for each of those audiences. You may have important contributions to make to inter- or multidisciplinary conversations. There will be times when you think a particular argument will be important for a particular audience but you are not yet confident that you are ready to communicate with them. Certain audiences will be more likely to listen to what you have to say if they know that your knowledge claims have been validated by a different audience.

Your first decision is what kind of publication would be most appropriate for the reader you are trying to engage. Some publishing tools are more suited to some purposes than others, and some audiences prefer different types of publishing tool. Communication among scholars is rather formal, and privileges highly literate forms like monographs and journal articles. Scholarly conversations are asynchronous and take place over very long time periods. They may involve dead people, or people who are no longer actively contributing to this particular conversation. The bar for acceptance into the conversation may be high. That said, scholarly conversations also include more informal or semi-formal modes of publication, including oral modes: in traditional formats like conference and seminar presentations, workshops, posters, working papers, and in newer media like blogs, podcasts, video, and multimedia presentations.

Think of "audience" and "readers" not as passive consumers of your knowledge but rather as actively engaging with your text in ways that you cannot completely control. Readers bring their own knowledge and experience to their reading of your publication, setting it in their own context. They bring it into conversation with work you may never have considered, if only in their own heads. Your reader may have read many of the texts you cite, but have interpreted them differently, or may be introduced to a body of work through your work. This will affect how they read your text. A reader encountering your article or book for the first time several years after it was published will read it in a context you could not imagine at the time of writing. Some readers may revisit the text several times, seeing new things in it or changing their opinion of it, because their personal intellectual context for your text has changed over time. You will only be aware of their readings of your work if they communicate with you directly or publish their own work and cite yours.

You are such a reader of the work of other scholars. Engaging in scholarly publishing will both communicate your ideas and arguments and contribute to your process of developing those arguments. Sometimes the timelines are short enough that those developments will appear in a publication you think of as a revision of the first publication; for example, when you use feedback on a conference presentation to revise your paper into a journal article. As your career progresses, you will notice that your engagement in these scholarly conversations—even in formal, asynchronous ways—has influenced the direction of your research and scholarship in ways that are evident in the types of contributions you are making now.

Readers judge books by their covers, literally and figuratively, and the publisher (in the broadest sense: the medium through which you make your work public) is an important piece of that cover. Your choice of publisher situates your work, and the specific conversation you invoke through your introduction, framing, and citations, in a wider conversation. It will have a significant influence on whether a reader finds your work, how the reader prioritizes your work in their own reading list, and how they read your work, with a consequent impact on the likelihood that your work will influence theirs.

If you plan to publish a book, your book will be considered in relation to other books with which it is associated. University presses have different associations than large commercial publishers in the minds of your readers (and evaluators). Large publishers have multiple imprints, all of which usually target different audiences and have different reputations. You may consider publishing in a book series with a series editor, connecting your work to the content and reputation of both the editor and the other books in the series.

Journal articles are part of a journal that has formed its identity over numerous issues and volumes. A journal article is also part of a specific issue, which may or may not be a themed special issue or a themed special section. Book chapters are part of a particular collection, which is then part of a series or list with a particular publisher or imprint.

Less formal publications will also be judged (by potential readers as well as by evaluators) partly by their context of publication: the specific conference in which you present your paper, and perhaps the stream or panel it is part of; the blog, podcast, or YouTube channel you choose to disseminate your work; the specific working paper series or online preprint archive you submit to.

A note for early-career scholars

Your early-career publications will draw substantially on your doctoral research, and may extend or enhance it, but they are no longer part of the dissertation project. Framing the publications that draw on your dissertation research as new publishing projects will help you forge a new identity as a qualified scholar and reduce the sense that your project is never-ending.

When creating an early-career publishing plan, there are multiple options available. You might publish either a monograph or a series of articles relatively quickly to communicate the main findings and arguments of the dissertation to a wider scholarly audience. You might then extend the same research programme and publish several further articles (or chapters) or a (second) monograph. In many fields, it will be reasonable to publish articles in your early career and only consider a monograph once you have a larger body of research to draw from.

Scholarly publishing and wider audiences

Your decisions about which specific publications to prioritize may also be influenced by your desire to engage with specific audiences outside of the academy (e.g. practitioners, policy makers, or those with a general interest in your topic), whose preferred mode of engagement is different from that of your scholarly readers. I encourage you to outline your options clearly, including their pros and cons for different audiences, and then set priorities based on the relative importance of different communication and validation goals at this specific stage of your career and research project.

If reaching a particular non-academic audience is important to you, you may wonder why you are publishing in scholarly outlets at all. How does scholarly publishing contribute to a communication strategy that prioritizes influencing policy, practice, or some other aspect of life beyond the academy? There are two ways that scholarly publishing is important to wider impact, even when your wider audience will not read your scholarly publications. First, the scholarly conversation is important to the production of knowledge useful to others. Second, the scholarly conversation validates knowledge—something you recognize whenever you argue for the importance of evidence-based policy or practice.

Research knowledge builds on earlier knowledge. As you refine your knowledge of your topic, you do so in conversation with other scholars working on related projects. The conversations you have among yourselves may seem esoteric beyond your group, but they are crucial to developing a solid knowledge base on which practices, policies, etc. can be built. Even in applied fields, your work may build on the less successful attempts of previous scholars. In this sense, the process of knowledge creation is collaborative even when you are not collaborating directly. Scholarly publication is the means by which you communicate with other scholars asynchronously.

In some fields, practitioners are eager to use research knowledge to influence their more practical day-to-day work. Highly qualified professionals in medicine, allied health professions, education, law, and social work are often aware that the research basis of their work is constantly changing. Any organization that wants to influence government policy or individual behaviour will also be interested in the relevant research. They may read (or at least intend to read) scholarly journals in the field to keep up with the latest knowledge. They may rely on other forms of publication designed specifically for their needs, due to time constraints or a preference for a different style of writing. Whether or not they read your scholarly publications, the fact that your knowledge has been validated by your peers is important to them, and may increase the chances that they will take your other forms of research communication seriously. If you produce separate publications for these audiences, citing your own scholarly publications will lend authority to the knowledge communicated and enable those who are interested to delve further into the research if desired.

Although you often have to publish differently to reach non-scholarly audiences, if practitioners in your field do read (or intend to read) scholarly publications, when you are selecting a specific journal you should consider how accessible it is to them. Some journals will assist in making shorter versions of the publication easily available to increase readership, despite the time constraints faced by specific professional audiences. (For example, some of the larger medical and scientific journals produce short videos or executive summaries of some of their scientific articles.) Open-access publications are likely preferable in this situation, not least because limited-access journals require financial resources or institutional connections that many of the non-academic audiences for your research do not have.

Commercial, scholarly, or open access?

While communication and validation are the major competing forces I see affecting scholarly publishing decisions, these are overlain with concerns about the business model of publishers themselves. As Aileen Fyfe and her colleagues point out, this is not particularly new, though it takes new forms in the twenty-first century:

> The ethos of the academic research community had historically been non-commercial, and the sharing of knowledge had historically been enabled by the generosity of publishing organisations—such as learned societies and university presses—with a mission for scholarship rather than profit. But since the end of the Second World War, academic publishing has become increasingly commercialised.

Political shifts have affected the funding of higher education, increased student numbers, and changed the nature of pressures to publish scholarly work. Changes in financial regimes within universities mean that many university presses have been restructured as separate commercial entities and required to make a profit. Scholarly associations, which are generally non-profit organizations, may also set up separate for-profit publishing entities as a way to generate funds, or even contract the publication of their journals to commercial or academic publishers in exchange for member benefits and wider marketing reach. These same pressures have also squeezed academic library budgets, making access to scholarly journals more difficult, even for those who are employed in universities.

The possibilities opened up by the digital revolution have complicated all of these issues. On the one hand, digital technology radically reduces (though does not eliminate) the costs of publishing. Many excellent scholars are working in institutions with limited financial resources. Political pressures to increase accountability for public funds seem to favour wider accessibility. On the other hand, both commercial pressures and the prestige economy of higher education resist a radical opening up of accessibility.

A detailed examination of the ethics and politics of choosing scholarly, commercial, or non-profit publishers, and of the various forms of open-access publishing, are beyond the scope of this *Short Guide*. While some scholars have taken the personal decision to only publish open access, and/or to boycott specific commercial publishers, this option may be too high risk for your particular circumstances. The focus on your communicative goals and how they intersect with the various evaluation processes you are subject to will provide a solid foundation for then considering the accessibility of your publications to different audiences, and the control over your copyright that you may need to ensure to compensate for limits to that accessibility when you make certain choices.

Because open-access publishing is relatively new, some of your senior colleagues may misunderstand it. I suggest that you use the starting points listed in the "Notes and further reading" section to learn more about open access so that you can weigh your specific options more carefully. These may include publishing with a fully open-access publisher, publishing an open-access publication with a hybrid publisher, or negotiating simultaneous or embargoed publication of an open-access version of a limited-access publication.

Other factors

When considering your publication options, you will also want to take into account the length of the contribution and whether you are going for depth or breadth of coverage. Consider also whether a single authorial voice would best communicate your argument or findings. This voice may be achieved by sole authorship or co-authorship. You may also have the option of juxtaposing multiple perspectives, either in one piece or by selecting an outlet that will put your contribution in the context of other perspectives.

Perhaps the most important consideration is ease of discovery by readers, an issue addressed in more detail in the final chapter. Consider particularly what type of reader a particular outlet will reach, how many readers, and where they are located. Ease of access to the full publication is a separate issue. Do not assume that ease of access is equivalent to ease of discovery.

The prestige of the outlet (for your intended audience) will make a difference to both whether a reader actually reads your publication and how they read it. Prestige is affected by the selectivity of the outlet and whether contributions are peer reviewed. Whether a particular form of publication is oral or written, and the extent to which some written forms embed characteristics of oral forms, also has an effect. That said, there are occasions when less-formal outlets are exactly what you need.

These criteria are addressed in relation to specific types of publication in the following chapters.

Some questions to consider

Begin by considering the readers you would like to engage with. Answering these questions does not commit you to actually publishing for any of the readers you identify; you are just being curious about who might benefit from the ideas you are writing about right now. You will refine your answers in the light of later chapters.

> Whose work has influenced the writing you have been doing?

> Who are you already (implicitly) talking to as you write? (It's okay if they are dead. Or famous. Or, equally, if they are not scholars, or not fashionable.)

> To whom would you like to say: "This is the work I've been doing; this is where I've got to; this is how it looks right now; how does it look to you?" (Dorothy E. Smith)

> Who would benefit from your work?

> Whose work or life would be better for knowing what you've been working on?

Don't think too hard about the above questions. Write down everyone that comes to mind. Write quickly, without stopping, until you run out of ideas:

very specific individuals (e.g. the author of another article)

scholars in a specific field (discipline, sub-discipline, interdisciplinary area)

a particular type of practitioner

general readers of particular kinds of books

Look at your initial responses and develop them further to get a better idea of your potential readers. Break down big categories into smaller ones. Expand individuals to consider them as a type. The following questions should help with this:

What types of publications do these readers value? What is the relative value to those readers of oral versus written forms? Is peer review important to them? How does the length of the publication influence this reader?

What broader conversations would you like your work to be part of? Where are those conversations happening in broad terms (e.g. conferences, journals, associations, imprints, series, websites, etc.)? What forms of publication are typical in those conversations?

Where are your preferred readers located, geographically and institutionally? How might that affect your choice of form and outlet?

What are your own views on copyright? Are you under any contractual obligation (e.g. institutional or funder policies) to make your publications open access? Considering your broader communication goals for this research project, what intellectual property rights do you need to keep?

Books

Book publishing is the norm in some disciplines (e.g. history, literature) and almost unheard of in others (e.g. economics, physics). (If your discipline is in the latter category, you can skip this chapter altogether.) There are several kinds of books you might write based on your scholarly work. Monographs, edited collections, scholarly editions, and textbooks are the most common types of book used in scholarly contexts. You could also consider creative nonfiction, children's books, poetry, or even fiction. Not all books communicate to the same kind of reader, and not all audiences read books as their primary way to learn things. Beware of assuming you are writing a book without really thinking about what that means, or whether another type of output would be more appropriate to your goals.

Books require more of a time commitment for your reader than other types of scholarly publication. In a discipline where books are common and expected, you can assume that your disciplinary colleagues will make time to read them. In a discipline where books are part of a more varied publishing landscape, length may factor into readers' decisions about what to prioritize. In either situation, ensuring a book is the right format for the specific knowledge you will be communicating increases the likelihood that readers will have good reasons to prioritize reading (and recommending) your book.

If other scholars are going to read and engage with your work, they first need to find it. All types of book are harder to find in database searches than journal articles because they are not indexed and abstracted in citation indexes like Web of Science (though reviews published in journals, and citations of books in journal articles, will appear there). The advent of Google Scholar, changes in the way publishers use metadata on their websites, and the ability to search the holdings of multiple libraries change the landscape somewhat, making it easier to search for books. Library acquisitions likely rely on the relevance of the book to the research and teaching interests of the institution at time of publication, making it difficult or impossible for scholars to access books that their own library did not purchase on publication. The advent of print-on-demand publishing means that books no longer go out of print, but academic publishers' pricing models may make print-on-demand versions of older books prohibitively expensive. If someone discovers your book several years after publication, they may face additional barriers to actually getting their hands on it. Open access book publishing addresses some of the concerns about availability but not those about discoverability.

I encourage you to consider who your desired reader is, whether they read books (and if so, what kinds of books), and why that reader should prioritize reading your book. Do this early in the process. Not only will it help you frame the project and make good decisions, but these questions are also central to the proposal you will submit to a publisher. The clearer you are about these questions, the easier it will be to choose prospective publishers and put together a strong proposal.

The sections in this chapter provide more details about the different book-related options for scholarly audiences in terms of content, audience, how they will be viewed in various validation processes, and how to select a publisher once you've decided a book is what you are writing. Although there are some situations in which creative nonfiction, fiction, poetry and other forms would be considered scholarly outputs, I have not discussed them in this *Short Guide* as they are usually written for wider audiences, even if based in your scholarship. I conclude with a section about book proposals and the fraught question of when you should secure a contract for your scholarly book.

I encourage you seek further information on the specific options you are considering. Talk to as many people as you can about specific issues they have experience or expertise in. You may do this over coffee or lunch. You may set up a short meeting by phone or video-call. You might do it by email. Respect their time by asking specific questions and keeping things as brief as possible. Your goal is to collect information that will help you make your own decision. If they recommend a particular course of action, ask them to clarify why they have made that suggestion. Thank them for their time.

Monographs

The monograph is a detailed written study on a single specialized topic. It is the obvious choice for depth of coverage. Monograph publishing is very common in the humanities and history, somewhat common in the social sciences, and almost unheard of in fields like economics or the hard sciences. In some fields, the monograph is almost essential to securing an academic career, or at least to progressing within one. It is likely that if you are a historian or a literary scholar and your career goals include a secure academic position, a monograph will need to be a priority, despite calls to change this practice.

Although monographs are typically single-authored, they may have multiple authors with a single authorial voice. A co-authored monograph should be considered a more advanced writing practice, and is probably not appropriate early on in your career.

The audience for your monograph will probably be scholarly; it will usually consist of other advanced scholars in your specific field, but may also include non-specialists interested in the topic and students on specialized courses. The primary audience will have a major impact on both the style and scope of the monograph. It is tempting to think that a scholarly monograph may speak to readers beyond your scholarly community. While it is true that a general educated reader is more likely to read a book than a scholarly journal article, their interests, background knowledge, and stylistic preferences make it very difficult, if not impossible, to write a monograph that will satisfy both audiences. The primary reader you have in mind will affect the content, writing style, and publisher you choose to approach. Hiring and promotion processes, especially in research-intensive institutions, may consider accessibility to wider audiences as diminishing the scholarly value of your book. Seek advice from senior scholars in your field in the types of institutions you would like to work in as you weigh the relative value of these different options at this point in your career.

Once you have decided that a monograph is appropriate and identified your primary audience, it is important to consider your choice of publisher carefully. The publisher will value commercial considerations, like the size of the market. Specialized scholarly monographs may thus be difficult to publish because they are likely to have a very limited readership (and thus sales). To your scholarly colleagues, this limited readership may be highly valued. This conflict means that publishers may encourage you to develop a different kind of book with a wider audience, perhaps taking you into generalist scholarly works in your (slightly less specialist) field, textbooks (perhaps for upper-level undergraduates, or even postgraduates), or scholarly books that might appeal to a broader non-scholarly readership. Be aware if the nature of the project is shifting, and make conscious decisions. It's your book. You get to decide.

Edited collections

Monographs are not the only form of scholarly book publishing. In some disciplines, especially those that also value monographs, edited collections are a common form of publishing short-form scholarship. An edited collection is a collection of short contributions (usually 6,000–10,000 words) on a single subject, each written by different authors, with a common theme and a structure that provides an overarching narrative. As such, an edited collection is designed as a coherent volume. The introduction and conclusion make connections between the various chapters and set the volume as a whole in the context of the wider conversation. The chapters themselves usually consist of multiple voices brought into dialogue—or debate. For example, the collection might bring together perspectives on a single topic from within a single discipline or across different disciplines, present academic research alongside policy or practitioner perspectives, or bring scholarship into conversation with other forms of writing (e.g. poetry, memoir, or short fiction). Edited collections can also introduce a range of scholarly work to a non-specialist audience through a shared interest in a particular topic. Some of these goals could also be achieved by publishing a special issue of a peer-reviewed journal.

As with any publishing project, consider how the form will affect how the reader engages with the content. The great advantage of an edited book (or a special issue of a journal) is that it foregrounds the sense of scholarly publishing as conversation. The work of the editor could be seen as shaping the conversation and situating the work as a whole in larger conversations. Individual contributions will be written and revised in relation to the other contributions and may also engage with other chapters directly. The whole is likely to be more than the sum of its parts, which may account for the way edited books are undervalued in validation processes that focus on the individual contributions (as editor or chapter author).

A collection may have a single editor or multiple editors. An edited collection may grow out of a small conference or workshop, editors may put out an open call for submissions, or some combination of the two. Editors might also extend invitations to specific authors for contributions to the collection. Authors selected might also be invited to an event to workshop their chapters before producing final versions. There are two ways in which edited collections can be part of your publication strategy: you can edit (or co-edit) such a collection, or you can contribute a chapter to such a collection. I will address the common issues first, and the issues specific to each in the following sections.

If your primary audience is other scholars, it is worth bearing in mind that, while writing a chapter for an edited collection may be similar to writing a journal article, and editing such a collection might be similar to compiling a special issue of a journal, edited collections have some drawbacks in terms of discoverability and validation processes compared to peer-reviewed journals. The reputation of the editor(s) may be significant in reaching an appropriate audience, with a subsequent effect on the significance of the contribution to the field. Some publishers find edited collections difficult to market and are therefore reluctant to publish them. And, unlike journals, the peer-review process for contributions to edited collections may not be well known or understood by your peers.

In addition to the general discoverability issues that apply to books, the individual contributions to an edited collection are not systematically indexed and abstracted in major databases, appearing in searches only when (and if) they are cited in publications that are indexed.

The time it takes for work to be discovered, read, and incorporated into an article where it is cited, and for that article to be published, introduces a significant time lag for chapter-level discoverability through citation indices. This means contributors are somewhat more dependent on the title and description of the collection, and the reputation of the editor and publisher, to find their readers. This is not necessarily a problem if your communicative goals align well with the communicative goals of the collection as a whole, but it does make it more difficult for secondary audiences for a chapter to come across it.

In validation processes, these issues with discoverability affect the evaluation of the likely significance of the contribution to knowledge. The press and editor(s) may be taken as a proxy for the quality of the contribution and the likelihood that it will have a significant impact on the advancement of scholarly knowledge. If you are being evaluated by disciplinary peers in a field where book publishing, including edited collections, is common, this will be less of an issue than if you are being evaluated by a multidisciplinary committee or in a discipline where journal articles are highly valued. These drawbacks are discussed further below, from the perspective of both editing and contributing to a collection. Journals, including special issues, are discussed in detail the next chapter (particularly in the section "Articles in the validation process").

Editing an edited collection

There are many good reasons to edit a collection but the work involved, and how it will be viewed in validation processes, differs considerably from writing a monograph. As the editor of a collection you will solicit contributions, ensure they are submitted, edit the contributions, get revisions back from contributors, write an introduction (and possibly your own contribution), secure a publisher, and manage the relationship with the publisher. As an editor, you will also be expected to advise on big-picture issues, and to provide feedback if a contributor is struggling with a chapter. While you may do less writing than you would for a monograph, the skills required are much more varied, and often time consuming.

The chapter level discoverability issues outlined above may influence the decisions of potential contributors. When researching publishers, ask acquisitions editors about chapter-level metadata. If your primary audience is scholarly, a special issue of a peer-reviewed journal can accomplish many of the same goals, and may be more appropriate, especially if you are in a discipline where book publishing is unusual. Publishing in a special issue also ensures all libraries that subscribe to the journal acquire your collection, that individual contributions are indexed in relevant databases, and that the scholarship cited in your collection will be captured in citation indices. The relative importance of these things will depend on your discipline and your communication goals. Special issues are considered in more detail in the next chapter.

In validation processes, an edited collection is not equivalent to a monograph. If you have been advised that you "need a book" for tenure or promotion, assume this means a monograph unless you have a clear indication to the contrary. Your own contribution to an edited volume will be valued—as any contribution to an edited collection would be—but an introduction may not be valued as highly as a contribution based on your own scholarship. Although your work as an editor adds scholarly value to the work, this is not well recognized in validation processes. It is more likely to be valued as an indication of the extent of your scholarly networks and your ability to collaborate, which may be important in certain contexts. The general considerations regarding audience, covered in the previous "Monographs" section, will also apply.

Contributing a chapter to an edited collection

From a contributor's point of view a chapter for an edited collection is about the same length as an article for a peer reviewed journal. Because edited collections are designed as coherent volumes, publishing in an edited book may also add value to your individual contribution through the larger themes and questions raised by its juxtaposition with the other contributions. The curated conversation of the edited book may facilitate your engagement with a particular audience. Such a contribution might be particularly well suited to bringing your work to a wider audience or to interdisciplinary debates. When considering contributing to an edited volume, you want to be clear about who the intended audience for the volume is and how that aligns with your own publishing goals.

The process of refining and submitting your work to an edited collection can also be less uncertain and stressful than an unsolicited submission to a peer-reviewed journal. You may be invited to contribute. Even if there is a call for contributions, the relatively narrow focus may make it easier for you to see how your work fits than the general scope of a journal. The editor(s) of the collection may provide considerable feedback on a draft or conference paper because they like your work enough to want to include your contribution in the volume. That said, a personal connection with the editor and other contributors may also make it more difficult to turn down such an opportunity if it does not align with your priorities.

As mentioned above, edited collections have some drawbacks in terms of discoverability compared to peer-reviewed journals. However, advances in publishing and search technology are improving discoverability, largely through the inclusion of chapter-level metadata in online book records. Publishers vary considerably in how they do this, and it is worth asking the editor(s) what arrangements have been made with the publisher for chapter-level metadata before making your decision to publish in a collection. Inclusion of your chapter in your own institution's repository may improve future accessibility (and may be compulsory for other reasons), so you should also confirm that the copyright arrangements will facilitate this.

Scholarly editions

In literary disciplines, one might also consider the critical or scholarly edition: an edition of a novel or other long-form primary work with an accompanying critical introduction, critical essays, and/or annotations. A critical or scholarly edition makes a significant contribution to advanced scholarship through attention to the textual and editorial history of the novel or work considered, and makes claims about what might be considered the authoritative version of the original text. The scholarly contributions to the edition may be made by a single scholar or by several scholars; in the latter case, an editor takes responsibility for the shape of the whole. Critical or scholarly editions are almost exclusively written with a scholarly audience in mind, though that audience may include students (especially those engaged in more advanced study). This type of scholarship is now commonly published in a hybrid digital–print mode, with further resources available digitally.

The scholarly edition should not be confused with an edition aimed at a general reader, nor with a teaching edition. Both of these types of book share some characteristics with the scholarly edition, but your peers in various validation processes will not value them in the same way. While the general reader may be interested in the text that is its focus, they are more likely to pick up a good regular edition—perhaps with a brief introduction, but without all the detailed scholarly apparatus. A teaching edition may include rather more scholarly apparatus than a general edition but will focus on introducing the main text to a novice scholarly audience, usually undergraduates. Audience and career goals will be important considerations as you contemplate your options.

To further complicate matters, the scholarly edition is almost completely unheard of outside a few literary disciplines. This can have serious consequences in inter- or multidisciplinary validation processes, including those awarding grants and fellowships, and even the stages of hiring and promotion processes that happen beyond your department. It may be important to explain the significance of this type of publication for the benefit of those unfamiliar with it in your promotion or application documents. If you serve on inter- or multidisciplinary committees that evaluate the scholarship of literary scholars, you will need to explain the nature and significance of the scholarly edition to your peers on the committee.

Textbooks

The fact that a book may be used in a classroom does not make it a textbook. Textbooks are specifically written to meet particular teaching needs. Textbooks usually summarize the state of current scholarship for a novice audience at a particular level; they often include study guides and other supplementary material, and companion test banks or other teacher resources. Some of this supplementary material may be provided digitally rather than in print. In literary disciplines, teaching editions of major works and anthologies of short works and excerpts would be in this category. In disciplines where books are a common form of publishing scholarly work, textbooks are less common at more advanced levels of study, with the possible exception of topics like theory or methodology. Textbooks may be more common in disciplines where books are not used to communicate among scholars.

Writing textbooks is a particular skill; one that requires bringing pedagogical knowledge to bear on your writing style and making careful decisions about the level of detail appropriate to the textbook's audience. The press is likely to have considerable input into decisions of structure and content, and may offer considerable editorial support. Due to the substantial market for textbooks, especially at sub-degree and lower-level undergraduate levels, textbook publishing is one form of scholarly publishing that can earn a not-insignificant income. While you may not earn your living this way, it may be worth considering as a supplementary income stream, especially if you also earn income from other activities that require similar instructional design skills. If this is your interest, you may also consider self-publishing and the growing rental market for textbooks.

There is also a growing movement for open-source textbooks and open educational resources, providing high-quality instructional materials using Creative Commons licensing with the ability to build on the work of others. Open-source textbook development is inherently collaborative on some level; those who might use the finished product have input into the form, even if only a few people undertake the major work of developing the initial textbook. If your institution has a Centre for Teaching & Learning or other unit that supports teaching development, they will be an important source of information and resources. There may be funding available from your institution or elsewhere to develop this kind of work.

The value of a textbook in various evaluation processes closely matches the value of the audience to those evaluating your published work. Your institutional location is crucial to making decisions here. In research-intensive institutions or institutions striving to improve their research reputation, textbook publishing is unlikely to carry much weight in tenure and promotion processes. It may even be considered an indication that you do not value the types of contributions the institution values, and are thus a poor fit. In teaching-focused institutions, or teaching-intensive positions within research-focused institutions, this kind of publishing may be highly valued as appropriate scholarship, and viewed as extending the impact of your teaching beyond your own classroom to influence the discipline/field more broadly. It is imperative that you consult with mentors in your discipline and institution.

Selecting a publisher for your book

Once you have decided what kind of book you want to publish, your next step is to select a suitable publisher. When researching possible publishers for a book with a primary audience consisting of other scholars, the presses that publish the books you and your colleagues read and cite are a good starting point. These will be familiar to your audience and your work is likely to fit well within their existing lists. If your book will extend your scholarly audience to other disciplines or interdisciplinary areas, consider presses with readerships that include all of your target audiences.

Acquisitions editors or series editors may approach you to consider publishing with them. Publishers attend conferences with a view to identifying interesting work that they might publish. Keep in mind that editors who invite you to submit a proposal are not making any promises. Until they've seen the proposal, you don't even know if the editor is imagining the same book you are imagining. Being invited to submit a proposal confirms that you are not the only person who thinks there is a readership for your work. You need to consider carefully which publisher is most likely to reach the readership you most want to reach. With the rise of self-publishing, several companies have arisen that appear to be publishers but are really "publishing services companies," which assist authors in the self-publishing process. Many of these are reputable companies, but many others charge high fees for low value. Properly considering all invitations you receive to submit ensures you are making conscious decisions about these issues.

As discussed earlier, readers judge books by the publisher and that publisher's list; they will be more likely to find your book if it is published by a publisher they are familiar with, and more likely to read it if they have enjoyed other books from that publisher. Some publishers commission series on broad topics and appoint a scholarly editor for the series. The reputation of the series editor and the other authors and books in the series will have an impact on the reception of your book. In validation processes, reputation often acts as proxy for likely reach and subsequent impact on knowledge in your field. There will be a hierarchy of presses in your discipline based on the reputation of both their peer-review processes and their reputation among scholars in your discipline. The alignment of your values with those of the press and those of whoever is evaluating your work is crucial.

Different publishers and imprints specialize in different types of books and reach different readers. Large commercial publishers often have both academic and trade arms, and perhaps different imprints within each of those broad categories. Smaller presses will be more specialized and may partner with presses in other countries for worldwide rights. There is a huge difference between a scholarly publisher that also tries to sell a few books to a wider audience and a trade publisher that also reaches a scholarly audience. Each will have a very different marketing strategy and a different reputation among the various audiences that you care about (including those evaluating your work for other purposes). Some publishers find edited collections difficult to market and are therefore reluctant to publish them.

You should also consider other details that may make a significant difference to your readers or to you as an author. Not all publishers routinely include an index, for example, though most scholarly readers find an index useful. Even if a publisher is willing to publish an index as part of the book, the policy on how the index will be produced may vary. Some publishers may consider hiring an indexer to be part of their publication costs. Some will be willing to hire an indexer on your behalf and have the costs reimbursed from your royalties. Others will expect you to arrange and pay for the production of the index yourself.

Policies on e-book, paperback, and hardback publication are also likely to vary, and may make a difference to your desired readership. Also consider the publisher's policy on copyright, open access, and depositing a preprint copy in your institutional repository (especially if this is a requirement of your institution, funding, etc.).

Supplement your knowledge of different presses as a reader by talking to colleagues and mentors who have already published books of a similar type to the one you propose to publish. Learn more about the process. Ask them what they wish they'd known before they signed their contract. Mentors who have experience as members of promotion or grant-review committees will have valuable advice about how specific publishers or series are seen in those validation processes. Colleagues at all career stages may have useful insights into the various parts of the process, what the publisher is willing to do to help you get the manuscript through the process, how much marketing support there is, and so on.

When to write a proposal and secure a contract for your book

Before you can publish a book, you need to write in a very different genre: the book proposal. Many scholars struggle with this, at least the first time they do it. While you may be used to thinking of your book in terms of its content, the proposal gives considerable weight to the issues highlighted earlier on in this chapter: Who is the intended reader? What is the contribution to knowledge? How does your book fit into existing scholarship on this subject?

As I explained in more detail in *The Scholarly Writing Process*, these questions are also crucial as you transition from satisfying your own intellectual curiosity about your topic to communicating your findings, analysis, and argument to others. You need to answer these questions yourself to make important editorial decisions about the structure and style of the book you are writing. There will be a point in your writing process when drafting a book proposal helps you clarify important issues and enables you to move the project forward. As such, while the book proposal is an output with a specific purpose—securing a publishing contract—you might also want to write one for your own personal use.

When you send a proposal to a publisher and secure a contract for the book depends on various factors, including your own personality, the demands of your career, and the nature of the book itself. If you are editing a collection, you will also need to consider the needs of your contributors and the importance of a contract with a publisher to meeting those needs. You will need to consider the project itself, your personal relationship to deadlines and external pressure, and the specific publisher's requirements.

Some publishers will not consider a proposal, especially from a new-to-them author, unless you can provide a complete manuscript. If the book you are proposing is a revision of your dissertation, they may consider the dissertation as a manuscript for this purpose, as long as the proposed revisions are clear in the synopsis section of the proposal. However, some publishers may require you to have completed the first round of revisions before submitting your proposal. Check the publisher's guidelines early on so you know their expectations. You can also ask about this if you are speaking to editors at conferences. If your preferred publisher requires a full manuscript but others do not, you will need to consider whether that changes how you rank the possibilities. Even if the publisher will accept a proposal earlier, there may be other good reasons to wait until you have a full manuscript before submitting one.

At certain stages of your career it may be helpful to have a contract, even if your agreed delivery date is a year or so in the future. In those fields where a monograph is expected for tenure, having a contract can be an important indicator of the likelihood of meeting that requirement, and may make a difference in hiring and annual review processes. An editor expressing interest in your book project and inviting you to submit a proposal (even if they express that invitation as "I would love to publish your book") is not a contract. A contract is a formal legal agreement that you have signed. Even though many contracted books are never written and deadlines frequently get extended (sometimes considerably), the fact that a press has given you a contract indicates to those evaluating your work that there is a book there. That said, if the more prestigious press for your project will not give you a contract until you have a full manuscript, it is probably not worth compromising just to obtain a contract. Your peers will also be familiar with this requirement.

Some scholars find that having a contract with a delivery date (even a negotiable one) and an editor makes it easier for them to sit down and write on a regular basis. A contract thus makes it more likely for this type of scholar to finish the book. Other scholars react to deadlines in the opposite way: the deadline generates resistance or rebellion, increasing the stakes for every writing session and making it harder to work consistently on the project. Others are somewhere in between. Similarly, some scholars find that having an editor to correspond with about potential changes to the argument and structure of the book helps them work through those phases of the project where it seems to be going in a different direction. Others find that they fight with themselves about necessary modifications for far too long in the (usually mistaken) belief that the contract requires them to write exactly what they proposed. Just because a colleague finds the contract and deadline reassuring doesn't mean that you will.

Quite apart from the influence having a contract and deadline will have on your writing process, different scholars' writing processes are different. You may need to write a substantial draft before you can be confident of the argument and structure of your book. If you are seeking a contract for a monograph based on your dissertation, you will have done this substantial drafting. If you are proposing a new book, or a substantial revision of your dissertation that includes new material, you may need to do some of that research and analysis (at least) before you can write a proposal. You may or may not call that "writing a draft", but you will probably need to write something to clarify the scope and purpose of the book for yourself. Writing a detailed outline and synopsis may be your normal starting point, and you may feel confident seeking a contract at that stage.

A further consideration, especially for those writing and publishing their first book, is how much confidence you have in how long your writing process will take. Many parts of the process are difficult or impossible to predict. Writing is not merely a process of transcribing knowledge from your head onto the page; it is simultaneously a cognitive process of articulating that knowledge. Once you have a full draft, you are more likely to be able to estimate how long revisions—even substantial ones—will take, and thus to propose a more realistic deadline. This is particularly important if having to extend your deadline (possibly multiple times) will send you into a spiral of self-doubt that will further slow your process.

Regardless of when you decide to submit your proposal, the review process leading up to a book contract should help you improve the project. If a publisher considers your proposal and sample chapters good enough to send out for review, they are already strongly committed to your project. Unless they come back with a strong refusal, the editor will likely help you figure out how to respond to the reviewers' comments to strengthen the proposal before issuing a contract. Similarly, once you have secured a contract, the editor may be willing to provide feedback on drafts and help you keep the project moving forward. It is certainly worth asking about the level of editorial support you can expect when you are making your initial queries prior to submitting a proposal.

Because reviewing a book proposal is a major undertaking, many presses will not send anything out for review that is under consideration with another press. Your initial queries prior to submitting a proposal should reveal whether it would be acceptable to submit to multiple presses simultaneously. You may need to rank your options and submit serially. If you do submit to multiple presses simultaneously, be transparent. Do not be surprised if a press that is interested in the proposal requests that you withdraw the book from consideration with other presses before they send it out for review.

Once you have an offer of a contract, seek advice from mentors about which elements of the contract are negotiable. For most academic authors, the most important issues to consider revolve around copyright. You license or assign copyright to a publisher for specific purposes. The publisher's opening position may be something like exclusive worldwide rights in all media in perpetuity. They will be willing to negotiate that down to something more reasonable.

Some questions to consider

Thinking about the topic you are excited about and the writing you've been doing:

> What form seems natural for the material you are considering?

> Is the book you want to write a detailed book-length study of a specialist topic? How specialized?

Or, is this the kind of topic where you want to juxtapose contributions from different perspectives, probably written by different contributors, such as by editing or contributing a chapter to an edited collection?

In terms of advancing knowledge, what would be the differences between publishing your material as a book or publishing it as part of an edited collection (e.g. comprehensive coverage, bringing different perspectives together, etc.)?

Are you certain about how the type of book you are considering writing, editing, or contributing to will be viewed in whatever validation processes most concern you at this stage of your career? If not, who could you ask for advice on this specific issue?

Turning to your potential audience:

Who is the reader you most want to reach? (Be specific. If scholarly, what kinds of scholars?)

What other readers might also be interested in this book?

Are there readers you think you should be writing your book for? Or that you may be required to write for to meet your career goals? Are they different from the readers you want to write for?

What stories are you telling yourself about writing for those audiences? Write them down so you can see them and address them. (These stories may or may not be true. You may need to do a bit of research to figure out if they are or not.)

What feelings came up as you read (and answered) these questions about the potential readership? Write them down so you can be aware of how they affect your decisions.

If you've identified more than one type of reader (e.g. different disciplines, scholarly and non-scholarly), consider the following questions for each type of reader:

Does this potential reader read (scholarly) books? What kind? For what purpose?

Why would this reader prioritize your book over other books or other means of acquiring knowledge?

How does this reader find out about new books? Are there particular presses that this reader is likely to go to for books?

If reaching a particular (type of) reader meant changing the style or structure of your book, and those choices would affect whether you reach one of your other desired audiences, would you make those changes?

If those choices would affect how those evaluating your publications for career purposes receive your book, would you make those changes?

If there are two different types of readers who you consider equally important, but who read different types of books and find them in different ways, do you think you have two books? Or is there another way you can reach one of those audiences and write a book for the other?

Keeping in mind your personal preferences and career goals, rank your intended audiences. Focus on the top two on this list. You cannot be all things to all people.

Considering what you've written in response to all of the previous questions,

What type of book do you think you want to write/edit?

If you are considering contributing to an edited book, are you certain this is the best place to publish your chapter? Do you want to review the next chapter of this *Short Guide* (on peer-reviewed journal articles) before making your decision?

Who do you hope to reach?

Do any particular publishers come to mind? List them. (No commitment, but this is useful information.)

When considering publishing with a specific press or contributing to a specific edited collection:

Have you heard of this press/editor? Have you read other things by this press/editor? If not, look up what else they have published, perhaps reading some abstracts or reviews.

Setting aside your insecurities about whether you are good enough, does it feel like your work fits with other things published by this press or with the approach this editor is taking to this volume?

Is this press/editor well known to the audience you most care about? Are their books regularly reviewed in journals this audience also reads? (In other words, are your readers likely to discover your work if you publish with this press/editor?)

(For edited books) Will the publisher be making chapter-level metadata searchable in the book record and on their website? How important do(es) the editor(s) think this is when you ask them about it?

Will the publication be open access (immediately or in the future)? What arrangements are there for depositing your contribution in your institutional repository? What else do you know about copyright arrangements?

How well do the answers to these questions align with your own needs vis-à-vis discoverability and your own values vis-à-vis access?

If you value communication beyond scholarly circles, what is the reputation of this particular scholarly conversation, press, or editor among those beyond the academy who you would like to take your work seriously?

Getting further advice:

Do you have colleagues who are more familiar with the particular scholarly conversation, press, or editor? What questions would you like to ask them to help guide your decision?

Do you have colleagues who have published with any of the publishers you are considering?

Do you have colleagues or mentors who have published the kind of book/chapter you would like to publish, even if it's in a different area?

Will any of the publishers you are considering be attending a conference you plan to attend? Can you make an appointment to meet with them?

Do you have colleagues who can help you clarify how the kind of book/chapter you would like to publish will be seen in the validation processes that matter to you? (Preferably those who have experience of being on evaluation panels.)

Peer-Reviewed Journals

Not all significant contributions to the advancement of knowledge are book length. In many disciplines, peer-reviewed journal articles are the norm. Your engagement with other scholars may be exclusively through journal articles, or your journal articles may complement your book-length contributions. The scope of the contribution made by a journal article is narrower than that of a monograph. Journal articles are typically around 6,000 to 10,000 words, although this varies; humanities disciplines typically tend towards the longer end of the scale and scientific disciplines towards the shorter. Peer-reviewed journals may also include even shorter contributions of various types, which may or may not be subject to the same peer-review processes.

Like monographs, peer-reviewed journal articles are a high-prestige form of scholarly publishing. This has implications for securing a readership, as well as for the various validation processes that concern you. In the hard sciences and some social sciences (e.g. economics), journal articles are the primary form of (high-prestige) scholarly publishing. In other disciplines, peer-reviewed journal articles, edited books, and monographs are all part of the publishing ecosystem.

As with any other publication, the audience is key to selecting an appropriate outlet for your contributions. An article goes beyond reporting a set of findings to make an argument that takes a stance in a specific scholarly debate. Your work may be relevant to different types of scholars. You may have contributions to make to different debates even within your own field. You may publish several articles from one research project, using your findings to contribute to different scholarly conversations. One advantage of shorter forms is that if you need to write in a different style or with a different focus for different readers, it is not as daunting (or time consuming) to write two articles as it is to write two books. It is also possible that some of the readers you want to reach prefer journal articles.

Peer-reviewed journals are the best scholarly outlet in terms of discoverability. Each article is indexed in major databases, usually with an abstract and keywords. Other scholars can find your work by searching subject keywords, your name (e.g. after hearing you speak at a conference), or by following a citation in another article. Libraries subscribe to the main journals in the fields relevant to scholars in the institution, often through consortia or other bundled deals with publishers, making articles accessible even if discovered many years after publication. While changes in commercial scholarly publishing have made it difficult for many scholars to access certain journals, they have also acted as a spur to the open-access publishing movement, which makes peer-reviewed journals more easily accessible (at least in electronic form). Open-access journals, along with various forms of pre- and post-publication archiving of articles in institutional repositories and other online archives, can make it easier for your reader to access your work. Even if the journal is not immediately accessible to them, other scholars will know your contribution exists and have a general sense of your argument from the abstract, and may be able to access it through interlibrary loan or the relevant institutional repository.

Typically, journal articles are submitted speculatively (without invitation), and the journal will have a process for selecting and refining submissions for publication. The editor or a member of the editorial board may make an initial selection based on basic criteria. Rejection at this stage is referred to as "desk rejection" because the manuscript has not gone out for detailed review. Submissions that pass this initial screening will then be sent out for scholarly peers with expertise relevant to the submitted manuscript to review. The reviewers will send detailed comments and a recommendation to the editor (or editorial board), who will make a decision and communicate it to you.

It is rare for a manuscript to be accepted without any revisions. A "revise and resubmit" decision may range from minor revisions until the editor is satisfied, to major revisions that will be sent back to the original reviewers, or to a combination of original reviewers and new reviewers; in rare instances, a manuscript may be treated as a new submission. Your submission may go through more than one round of revision before final acceptance and publication. Some journals will also require several rounds of revisions after acceptance. Your submission may be rejected outright after peer review (and even after a round of revision). Unless there is a clear and unequivocal statement from the editor that they would welcome a new submission on this topic, you should not resubmit a revised version of a rejected article to the same journal.

Journal articles may be sole authored or have multiple authors. Conventions around authorship and the order in which multiple authors are listed vary by discipline. Your scholarly association may have ethical guidelines for authorship. It is advisable to clarify the principles you will be using early in the process of writing a co-authored article for publication. Meaning may be attributed to author order in validation processes. If there is no fixed convention in your discipline, you should specify the criteria used to determine author order in a footnote. One author will take responsibility for corresponding with the journal about your submission; this may or may not be the first author. If your manuscript is rejected and you submit to a different journal, you may change who takes on this responsibility. If your name will appear as an author, you should read the final draft before submission to be certain you are willing to be associated with it.

Submitting to a peer-reviewed journal is daunting. You have to make judgements about both the suitability of your article for this particular journal and its quality. You risk rejection, which is difficult for everyone. The quality of review and the care taken to communicate criticism constructively varies considerably, creating more emotional work down the line. It is unsurprising that you feel some resistance to submitting your work. Getting feedback from known and trusted mentors can help, both before submission and when you receive reviewer comments, but will not eliminate the difficult emotions entirely.

Special issues and special sections

Occasionally a journal will publish a special issue or special section on a specific topic. Special issues can come about in a variety of ways. The editors may have noticed a theme among submissions and decide to publish them together to increase the impact of the journal in that area. If the journal is associated with a scholarly association, they may regularly publish a special issue associated with the association's annual conference to showcase key themes. Guest editors might propose a special issue on a specific topic as an alternative to an edited book (see the previous chapter for a discussion of the pros and cons of editing, or contributing to, an edited collection). There may be a call for papers inviting submissions for consideration. In some cases, submissions will be invited directly based on professional networks or a conference or workshop presentation. In addition to the discoverability benefits brought by the journal itself, the special issue adds value to your article through its association with other articles in the issue or section.

Such special issues or special sections may or may not use the journal's usual peer-review process. The selection process may be more rigorous, perhaps incorporating an extra layer of review to ensure the issue as a whole works together; or it may be somewhat less rigorous, relying on the guest editors' selection process. Extra support may be available to refine your submission so that it meets the standards necessary to publish it. This extra support may take the form of a writing workshop for a group of scholars whose work is selected for inclusion, or comments on a draft from the editor. Sometimes, articles submitted in response to a call for papers for a special issue may be rejected from the special issue but accepted for review for the general issues of the same journal. If you are considering submitting an article to a special issue or special section of a journal in response to a call for papers or an invitation from the editors, it is a good idea to confirm what the process will be. If a call for papers for a special issue speaks directly to your research area but you are not yet ready to submit something, keep the journal in mind as a possible venue for publishing future articles.

Contributions to journals that are not full-length articles

Some peer-reviewed journals have separate sections for contributions shorter than the standard article. These sections often focus on methods or early dissemination of results, and are often called something like "Research Notes". Some journals may occasionally publish sections with shorter research-based responses to current events as a way of bridging the divide between research and policy or practice. While likely to be less highly regarded than full-length articles in validation processes, these types of shorter contributions may be important for publicly staking out your area of research in a highly competitive research field, and for making early contributions to debates based on your research data. They may also be a suitable way to make a small contribution to debates outside your main field. Familiarize yourself with previously published articles in that section of the particular journal for a sense of the style and approach. Never assume that the peer-review process for these sections is the same as for standard article submissions without checking. Sometimes it is. Sometimes there is an expedited review process (e.g. to publish work that speaks directly to current events). Sometimes there is a different process altogether for a particular section. If the process is not clear in the submission guidelines, contact the editor to clarify.

Many humanities and social science journals, especially those associated with scholarly associations, also publish book reviews and review articles. A book review will be a relatively short summary and critical evaluation of one book. The journal will usually have received books for this purpose from publishers and will pass them on to reviewers. Single book reviews are unlikely to go through a peer-review process, though the editor or member of the editorial board may request revisions prior to publication. Review articles normally deal with several books on a theme, providing a critical evaluation that goes beyond individual contributions to consider the books in relation to each other. You may be invited to undertake one and provided with the books, or you might propose one to the editor(s). A review article may be a similar length to a standard article and undergo a similar peer-review process. It is prudent to verify what the process is.

If you are considering making any of these types of contributions to a peer-reviewed journal, it is a good idea to verify discoverability. The prestige of the journal affects readership and audience reach, even for lower-status contributions to the journal. Do a quick search of a few past contributions to the section to see how they appear.

Do individual contributions get indexed separately, or is the whole section indexed as a block? Are there abstracts? If there are citations in the short pieces, do they appear in a citation index search of the work cited?

Selecting a journal

When deciding to publish a journal article, deciding between publishing in a journal and accepting an invitation to publish in a special issue or edited book, or deciding whether to publish an edited book or propose a special issue for a journal, the specific journal matters. Begin with your audience. Peer-reviewed journals are primarily read by other scholars. Be specific about which scholars you want to reach and which conversations you are contributing to. Identifying the journals in the field in which those debates are happening should give you a manageable list of options, which you can then rank. Your own reference list is a good place to start.

Journal editors (and publishers) have a strong sense of the purpose and scope of a journal that will encompass the subject matter covered, appropriate methodologies and theoretical frameworks, and style of writing. Although journal articles are often read as stand-alone pieces, with little attention paid to their relationship to other articles in the same issue or the journal as a whole, it is important to consider the journal as a coherent publication. While journal editors recognize that their journal does not have a monopoly on a particular scholarly conversation, they care very much about its collective contribution to particular debates and expect articles they publish to be in conversation with other articles in the journal. This is not just about citation metrics and their own validation processes. It is about the role of the journal as a whole in advancing knowledge in a field.

Titles and general descriptions are appropriate for a first pass at narrowing down your options. Look more closely at those that seem well suited to determine what the important criteria might be for "fit" and decide whether those are things you already do or could reasonably do. Look through a few issues to get a sense of the type of work they publish and the style of writing. Does your research approach feel out of place among the work published over the past several issues? Has any of the work you cite been published in this journal?

Give serious consideration to the probability that other scholars will find your article, read it, and take it seriously. Although most scholars will do a comprehensive database search for relevant material at some point in a project, this is not the only way that scholars find new articles to read. Many will have favourite journals that they routinely look at for new work in their field, which means the reputation and circulation of particular journals can make a difference to reaching your intended audience. Furthermore, some scholars will use journal reputation as a filter for their to-read list as a way to manage both the volume of new publications in their field and the limited time they have available to read.

Once you have a list of journals that will reach your desired readership, consider the specifics of the validation processes that are important to you at this stage of your career. If you know that those evaluating your body of work will use journal impact factors, then find out what those are (no matter how flawed) and include them in your decision-making process. It is also worth considering the relative value of making a significant contribution to a relatively small area (a sub-discipline, or a very specific debate within your field) compared to making a minor contribution to a debate of wider relevance within your discipline. The value of contributing to interdisciplinary debates or debates in a different discipline based on your research should also be carefully considered. Most validation processes will consider your publications collectively in determining the significance of your work, so this may be a matter of your overall publication strategy and how the choice of journal for this particular article fits into it.

Be aware that there is now a recognized problem of journals that take advantage of those who focus on validation issues by charging high fees to publish in journals of questionable quality. The exact definition of a predatory journal is somewhat contested. Publishing with such a journal will achieve neither your communication nor your validation goals. Furthermore, such a publication may actively damage your reputation. Be cautious about unsolicited communications from journals inviting submissions. Remember, unsolicited submissions are the norm. Most journals do not actively solicit contributions outside of special issues. Seek advice from specialist librarians and senior scholars in your field prior to submission.

Consider your own values around copyright and accessibility, as well as any requirements of the research funder. What are the copyright arrangements? Are any of your options open access? Do they have options for making individual papers open access? How do they handle the requirements around institutional repositories?

You may also want to consider how well the journal is managed, especially if you are under pressure to publish within a specific timeframe. Some journals publish information about the average time from first submission to acceptance. Your colleagues may have experience with particular journals as authors, reviewers, or members of the editorial board, and may be willing to give you guidance about how well that process is managed. A group in the Netherlands, scirev.org, manages a database of such information, which you can consult and contribute to. Colleagues may also share their experiences with particular journals.

If you are at an early stage in your scholarly publishing career, aiming to reach an audience you have not published for before, or targeting a journal that feels like a stretch in relation to your previous publishing, it is a good idea to speak with a trusted mentor who is part of the audience you want to reach. They will be able to give you advice about the suitability of the journal and any specific things you need to address. If validation issues are important to you, also check with a mentor who is familiar with the specific processes you are concerned with to ensure you are not misinterpreting how an acceptance by this journal will be viewed.

Your objective is a ranked list of two or three journals. Having a specific journal in reserve in case of rejection makes it easier to deal with the fear of rejection. Prepare your article for the first journal on your ranked list. Final revisions to your article should ensure that your style suits the journal to which you are submitting and engages with relevant work published by that journal. It is very rare for manuscripts to be accepted without revisions. Peer review acts as a form of formal feedback ensuring the high quality of the articles published. You are aiming for a revise and resubmit decision, with useful feedback from the expert reviewers. You need to judge whether your draft is finished enough for submission: is it worthy of the reviewers' time and goodwill, even if there will be further revisions based on their feedback? Early in your career, and whenever you are publishing for an audience you are less familiar with, it is a good idea to ask for feedback from a more experienced colleague before submission. Accept that outright rejection (even desk rejection by an editor without sending it for review) is a learning experience and will hone your judgements in future.

Overlap between articles and books, and between articles

For those who also publish monographs, fear that publishing shorter contributions to knowledge will make your book-length work unpublishable (or unoriginal) affects publishing decisions. This is one occasion where writing a book proposal can be helpful. (See section "When to write a proposal and secure a contract for your book" in the previous chapter.) The clearer your sense of the book, the easier it will be to identify articles and chapters that do not threaten its viability. However, it is not uncommon to publish one or two shorter pieces as you are working out the argument that will eventually become a monograph, and some presses may even expect this. I advise you to speak to editors at presses you are likely to publish with to get a clearer sense of how that determination might be made. Also check with journal editors to ensure that the copyright arrangements for articles would allow future publication as part of a larger work. Other scholars in your field may also have good advice, especially if they publish both monographs and journal articles.

Broadly speaking, an article that summarizes the book's main argument could provide a useful introduction to the main argument and entice scholars to read the book for more detailed and nuanced arguments and evidence, improving discoverability and readership for the longer version. If reading your article makes reading the whole book pointless, then you need to question whether there really is a book-length project. Similarly, stand-alone articles that become chapters of a longer work will take on new meaning in the context of the book, as long as the previous publication is acknowledged appropriately. It is also worth considering whether an article and a monograph chapter are indeed the same if the framing is different; for example, if it is addressing a different type of reader and contributing to a different (wider or narrower) debate. Consider your communicative goals carefully and ensure that any overlap in publications is appropriately acknowledged in each.

This issue is part of a larger concern about self-plagiarism: the reuse of substantial portions of text in multiple publications with the intention of deceiving the reader (or publisher) regarding its originality. A full discussion of the ethics of self-plagiarism and self-citation is beyond the scope of this *Short Guide*. Consult the research integrity policies of your institution and scholarly association for guidance. If you are focused clearly on your communication goals in making publishing decisions, you should be able to articulate how a particular article makes an original contribution (and thus differs from other things you have published in a similar area). I also strongly encourage you to formally acknowledge related work through self-citation, acknowledgements, or a combination of the two.

Articles and chapters in the validation process

The differences in both the level of peer review and the discoverability of journal articles affect how they are seen in validation processes. In general, standard-length articles in peer-reviewed journals are considered the highest status. The high level of discoverability increases the possibility that your work will have an impact on the work of others in your field.

In most situations, the adjudication committee will not read your work but rather will rely on what they know about the journal in which it is published to establish the quality and likely impact. The fact that your work has already been evaluated by peers and found to meet acceptable standards of rigour and contribute to knowledge means the peers evaluating you for hiring, promotion, funding, or whatever can trust the judgement of those other peers. What those evaluating your publications really care about is the significance of the impact on the advancement of knowledge. This is notoriously hard to judge, especially over the short term. They may use citations of your work as an approximate measure. However, most evaluation processes happen long before it would be reasonable to see much actual impact of that type.

Journal impact factors and other statistical measures are an attempt to predict the likely future impact (as measured by citations) of articles published in a particular journal. The relative importance of this kind of quantitative measure of journal quality and impact varies considerably by discipline. Journal impact factors are highly problematic, especially in fields with significant publishing outside of indexed journals, and tend to favour established journals over newer ones, among other things. Even where quantitative measures are not used, more qualitative or subjective rankings of journals may be used in practice. (See section "Indicators of impact on the advancement of knowledge" in the first chapter "What is publishing and why do it?" for more details about why this is difficult.)

In terms of quality, the things that make submitting to a peer-reviewed journal daunting are also the things that make a publication in a peer-reviewed journal more valued by your scholarly peers. Competition is assumed to weed out lower-quality work, which leads to greater value being given to publications in journals with a higher rejection rate and valuing unsolicited submissions over special issues. The peer-review process for unsolicited submissions to journals is generally well known and understood by your peers.

Not all publications in peer-reviewed journals have the same status. Special sections (and special issues) suffer from a lack of certainty about the peer-review process. Shorter pieces with a limited remit may also be assumed to make a relatively less significant contribution. The audience for that section of the journal is crucial to determining whether such pieces will be considered a contribution to knowledge, and what kind of contribution. Although they may be of lower value in the validation process, this type of publication may have value for other reasons; for example, staking a claim to a line of enquiry that will also result in longer contributions at a later date. As such, these publications may indicate a possible future trajectory that is important to the committee evaluating your work.

Review articles, especially those with a significant critical analysis, may be considered a research contribution, though perhaps not of the same level as a research article. If review articles go through the same peer-review process as standard articles for that journal, that will make a difference. Having been invited to write a review article will likely be seen as evidence of your reputation in the field. A book review is usually considered a service to the profession rather than a research contribution. Reviews improve discoverability of monographs and edited collections, and provide important evidence of the quality and impact of publications for the authors' and editors' own validation processes. If you work in a discipline that values books, and are likely to publish books yourself, writing book reviews is a form of diffuse reciprocity. On a personal level, book reviews can be a good incentive to read books that are relevant to your research or teaching.

Some questions to consider

Is there an article-length contribution to be made?

Is there an obvious scholarly conversation you are engaging within this piece? Where is that conversation happening? (How have you already situated your argument? Who have you cited? Where are the things you've cited published?)

Which scholars would you like to read and engage with your work (individuals or types)? Why would they be interested? What work of theirs does it relate to?

Where do those scholars publish their work?

Is this contribution engaging with a conversation that is active right now in which other participants are also seeking to publish work? Would a special issue, bringing that work together in one place, enhance the individual contributions? Would situating your work alongside others doing related work help you collectively establish a new scholarly conversation?

When considering a specific journal:

Have you heard of this journal? Have you read other things in this journal?

Skim the table of contents and abstracts for the past few issues. Setting aside your insecurities about whether you are good enough, does it feel like our work fits?

What are the length requirements? Do they suit your article?

Do you have (a) colleague(s) who is more familiar with the particular scholarly conversation or journal? What questions would you like to ask them to help guide your decision?

Are you certain about how different options for this publication will be viewed in whatever validation processes most concern you at this stage of your career? If not, who could you ask for advice on this specific issue?

If you are considering a lower status contribution (e.g. a short research note), how might this publication contribute to your longer-term communicative goals (e.g. stake a claim, make an initial foray in a new field)?

Will the publication be open access (immediately or in the future)? What arrangements are there for depositing your contribution in your institutional repository? What else do you know about copyright arrangements?

How well do the answers to these questions align with your own needs vis-à-vis discoverability and your own values vis-à-vis access?

Publishing Work in Progress

All of your publishing cannot be high-status publishing. Conferences, seminars, working papers, classrooms, and blog posts are ideal publishing venues when you are in the earlier stages of developing your arguments, even if their status in validation processes is lower. In many of these venues, you can be less authoritative, more tentative, and invite questions, suggestions, and discussion. While there is concern in some fields that such publications may enable others to "scoop" you, it is equally likely that this kind of work-in-progress publication provides concrete evidence that you were either working on the project simultaneously or that you were in fact the first to do so.

Although it is not the focus of this particular *Short Guide*, some of the forms discussed in this chapter may also be well suited to reaching non-academic audiences. Blogs, videos, podcasts, public talks, etc. may have lower status within academia but may be important for other communicative goals. I do not intend to discourage you from publishing in these ways, but rather to ensure that you are clear about how those evaluating your work in academic contexts will (or will not) value those outlets, so you can make choices consistent with your goals.

The types of publication discussed in this chapter may be used to seek feedback as you develop your ideas, and to open up scholarly conversation in a less formal way. While the impact of this type of publication may be limited, it builds an audience for your more formal (and higher-status) publications. The audience may be small, but that small audience can give you an immediate sense of the impact and quality of your arguments.

Success in this context means you engage others with the ideas you are writing and thinking about, and generate ideas for how you can further develop your work on this subject, either as a revision of this particular piece or as additional projects. Success may also be in long-term impact that is more difficult to see. Those who have heard your conference presentation or read your blog post may keep an eye out for the journal article. When they see the formal publication, they may move it up their to-read list because they remember how interesting the work in progress was. The networks you build through these forms of publication may lead to invitations to contribute to edited collections or special issues of journals, or to collaborate on research projects.

In formal validation processes, everything covered here tends to be seen as an indication of a pipeline of work that will be published in the future and of the scholarly communities to which you belong. Early in your career, this type of publication is a way of signalling work in progress. As you advance in your career, the relationship between these types of publication and more formal ones will be more obvious, and will enable those evaluating your work to imagine more clearly where it might go next.

That said, the relative value of written and oral communication affects the status of various forms of work-in-progress publication, and there are outlets that are more or less reputable. Oral forms, including conference presentations, have lower status that written ones. However, having a presentation or working paper accepted in a more prestigious outlet will have some influence over validation processes, if only to suggest that your chances of publishing in prestigious journals or with prestigious presses is higher. Research on digital communication in scholarly networks suggests that certain online forms of publishing may be tainted by their similarity to oral communication. Oral and digital forms have an important place in the ecology of publishing for scholarly audiences but, to have value in the various validation processes, must be part of a strategy that also includes written, preferably peer-reviewed publication. Seek advice from mentors with recent experience of editing journals to clarify how the written artefacts of oral scholarly communication (including repositories of conference papers) will affect your ability to publish a peer-reviewed journal article based on the same work.

Conference papers and posters

Conference papers and posters have been an important part of the ecology of scholarly publishing for a long time. Having people in the room feels more like you have a "real" audience in comparison to unknown (and feared non-existent) readers of your articles and books. Some conferences (or panels within conferences) may encourage explicit engagement between presenters, perhaps using a roundtable or workshop format. All conferences offer the opportunity to continue discussions more informally.

Despite the shorter length, more informal nature, and lower status of conferences, this type of publication can be more difficult to write. The constraints are quite severe, requiring you to focus on your own contribution to the debate with little time to delve into the context in which it is situated. You may need to write the longer version with the full context to reassure yourself that you can discuss the context in more detail if asked. Keep your communicative goals in mind. Consider the audience you would like to reach and select conferences and panels accordingly. By presenting your paper or poster, you have already succeeded in the goal of staking a claim to this small contribution to the scholarly conversation. If you would like to receive particular types of engagement or feedback, you can explicitly invite those kinds of comments when you present. Everything else contributes to your understanding of the conversation to which you are contributing and will help you make decisions about how to take this work forward.

Facing criticism in person and in real time can be daunting, especially if thinking on your feet is not one of your strengths. Having your interlocutor (whether critical or supportive) standing in a room several feet away from you and expecting an immediate response is quite different from receiving written comments, which you can set aside and return to or ask for assistance with. Use whatever strategies you have to centre yourself before presenting and before answering a question. Taking a few deep breaths before responding to a question usually comes across as thoughtful and doesn't take anywhere near as much time as your gremlins think it does. You can even jot down a couple of keywords before you speak. You are not required to convince anyone of the rightness of your position. Not all questions and comments require a response. You can make a note, thank them for raising that point, and suggest that you will consider it more carefully as you move forward with your project. In some cases, you may even want to suggest that you would welcome a longer conversation outside of this particular session.

While many conference attendees are considerate and work hard to ask interesting questions or raise important issues in constructive ways, there are some who are self-centred, rude, or hostile. The chair of your session may or may not be helpful in managing this. If a question or comment feels like a personal attack, remind yourself that the person asking the question feels insecure in their own position, even if they are in a much more secure or high-status situation than you are. Respond politely and indicate to the chair that they should move on to the next question.

Being invited to give a keynote presentation at a workshop or conference is a different type of activity. This type of presentation may outline the state of the debate as an introduction or conclusion to a broader range of contributions to be made during the conference itself. A keynote might also be a showcase for what is considered exemplary work in the field. The length of the presentation is likely to be longer, the audience larger, and the impact greater than a contribution to a regular conference panel.

Conferences in the validation process

In general, conference presentations are lower status than journal articles or book chapters. Their importance lies in signalling that you have work in progress that is reasonably well advanced, and situating you in a scholarly community. Some conferences in some disciplines peer review contributions; those conferences will likely be of higher status. Peers in your discipline who serve on evaluation committees will be familiar with the main conferences in your field and their practices, and will know the extent of peer review a conference paper is likely to have received. Peer review of conference papers should not be confused with a process for selecting papers based on abstracts. The latter is not peer review and should not be indicated as such in your CV or publication list.

The status of a keynote presentation will be closely related to the status of the event and the specific role of the keynote presentation within the event. At the very least, having been invited to give a keynote presentation will be seen as an indicator of the esteem in which your contributions to the debate are held.

Some conferences publish proceedings. There may also be an online repository of conference papers. The status of conference proceedings (or digital repositories of conference papers) will vary, as will peer-review practices. Your contribution may be peer reviewed either before acceptance to the conference or between the conference and the publication of proceedings. Check with senior mentors in your discipline to determine the status of such proceedings in relation to peer-reviewed journal articles. It is worth checking whether a publication in proceedings or depositing your paper in a repository affects what can later be submitted to a peer-reviewed journal.

Discoverability of conference presentations is poor. There is some informal circulation of copies by request, but the difficulty of acquiring a copy increases over time. Published proceedings and repositories increase discoverability, but be sure to verify how easy it is for potential readers to find articles in the proceedings in database searches. It may be difficult for those who come across a conference paper later to determine whether substantial changes to your argument or evidence were made following the conference, reducing the likelihood your conference paper will be cited or recommended to others. A more likely outcome is a further search for a version formally published in a book or journal.

Be very careful. There is now an acknowledged problem of predatory conferences, scams to extract money through an appeal to your need to present your work for validation purposes. You may receive flattering invitations to conferences that sound legitimate but are often not really conferences at all. If you attend, you risk not only wasting time and money but also your reputation. Check with trusted colleagues and mentors, especially early in your career or when considering presenting to an audience with which you have little experience. The academic integrity office of your institution, your research librarian, and your scholarly association may also have resources for identifying legitimate conferences in your field.

Working papers and preprints

In some disciplines, written forms of work-in-progress publishing have a considerable history. For example, economics has a longstanding tradition of publishing working papers. Working paper series may be published by a range of organizations, from individual departments to research networks or centres, some of which are quite prestigious. At one time they would have been photocopied (or even mimeographed) sheets; now, they are likely to be distributed as PDF files. Similarly, some scientific disciplines now have well-established electronic preprint archives. Typically, preprints are submitted to the archive at the same time a manuscript is submitted to a peer-reviewed journal.

The shift to digital circulation of working papers has likely improved discoverability considerably, though some of the older mimeographed (and later photocopied) series did circulate widely. Because of this, working papers and preprints now seem to be primarily a way of speeding up the conversation between peers that is so crucial to the advancement of knowledge, while acknowledging the importance of the peer-review process to ensuring the quality and validity of findings. Check with mentors in your field regarding the etiquette surrounding acknowledgement and citation of the working paper in a subsequent publication in a peer-reviewed journal.

In validation processes, the working paper itself is unlikely to count as a publication, though the reputation of the series may be taken as evidence of the quality of your work, your likelihood of publishing in high-status journals in future, and the quality of your networks. Publication in a working paper series may also serve to stake your claim to a particular line of argument or analysis prior to more formal publication. A reputable preprint archive or working paper series will increase discoverability of your work and enable other scholars in your field to engage with your work right away, even if the peer-review process takes some time. There is some evidence to suggest that submitting a paper to a preprint archive increases citations of the peer-reviewed version once it is published. It seems likely that you might get citations of the peer-reviewed publication earlier, because those familiar with your ideas need only check that the earlier version is consistent with the published version. Practices may vary by discipline, so it is always best to confirm with mentors in your own discipline and those familiar with the specific validation processes that concern you at this stage of your career.

Invited seminars

Many institutions have a regular research seminar series in which scholars are invited to present work in progress for discussion. Geographic and budget considerations may constrain the frequency of such events and who can be invited. Although there are a few high-status lectures and seminar series, by and large these should be considered as opportunities to present your work to a small group of interested colleagues, broaden your network, and obtain interesting feedback on your work. It is acceptable to let people know that you will be in the area for other reasons and would be available to give a talk. You might also ask mentors or colleagues to introduce you to people you would like to establish a scholarly relationship with. The work of maintaining relationships with mentors and colleagues in other institutions should include informal updates on work in progress so that they are in a position to recommend you as an alternative if they decline an invitation.

In this context, your presentation is likely to be considerably longer than a conference paper, and the focus of the discussion will be your paper. This makes such seminars an excellent way to engage in dialogue with colleagues and get feedback on your work in progress. However, increased pressures on academics' time has resulted in a decline in attendance at regular departmental seminars, which can be disappointing for all concerned.

In evaluation processes, the value of the paper itself is primarily as an indication of a pipeline to future publications. Discoverability of the work by those not in attendance is poor, and highly dependent on whether the host institution advertises the seminar on their website and keeps a record of past seminars on their website. The fact of having been invited indicates your esteem among colleagues in your field and provides an indication of the networks to which you belong. The presentation may also build an audience for the future formal publication, which is likely to increase its impact on the advancement of knowledge.

Blogs, podcasts, videos, etc.

The influence of technological innovation on scholarly publishing is already evident in the proliferation of online journals (commercial and open access), institutional repositories, preprint archives, and so on. All of these are variations on established modes of scholarly communication, potentially increasing discoverability and broadening the reach of scholarly communication beyond the academy. However, technological innovation has also brought new ways of communicating with scholarly peers through blogs, podcasts, and social media.

Unlike working papers and preprints, academic blogs are generally much shorter-form publishing with a much more informal style of writing. A thousand words is considered a longish blog post but is very short in relation to a peer-reviewed article. A blog post necessarily has a narrower focus. It can be a good place to write more thoughtful notes about reading or specific bits of evidence. You can also use a blog to summarize longer forms of writing about your scholarly work to generate interest. You might consider using podcasts or video in a similar way.

An academic blog may exclusively focus on research; barely touch on research in favour of teaching, policy, or other issues; or cover a wide range of types of post. Blogs may be individual or collective. Some may be formally associated with particular institutions (e.g. a funded research project, or a research centre). There is considerable variation in how well researched a blog post is and in how carefully a blog references other work. Some blogs will welcome guest posts from scholars who do not normally publish in this way. Some scholars will blog, podcast, or whatever regularly. None of these variations are bad in and of themselves. You will make choices regarding this type of publication based on your own needs. Your approach to blogs, podcasts, and videos may change over time, and needs to be considered carefully in relation to your own communication and career goals.

Blogs, podcasts, video, and social media are not well understood by those evaluating your work for scholarly purposes, and are unlikely to be valuable in validation processes. They are basically self-published, not peer reviewed, very short forms, and those on a committee must make a considerable effort to even determine how valuable they might be. You are likely to have to educate your evaluators about the particular features of your own publishing in this form, providing evidence of how it meets criteria they value, in a way you would never have to do for more well-established forms of publication. At best, these formats are likely to be equivalent to conference papers, in that they show a pipeline of future publications and generate interest in your work that might result in your more formal publications having more impact. If you blog about teaching and are in a teaching-focused position or institution, this may be valuable to indicate self-reflection and innovation in your teaching practice and influence on scholarly debates about teaching. If your institution values communication with wider audiences, it may be valuable in evaluating your impact beyond the academy, providing you have solid evidence of engagement (at least) and impact.

Despite the uncertainties around how newer forms of scholarly communication may be seen in validation processes, blogging, video, podcasting, and social media may have an important effect on your own writing process. While some find (or fear) that blogging will take time away from other more valuable activities, others find it helps their writing process and makes them more productive overall. As Rohan Maitzen pointed out in one of her posts:

Blogging has helped me get comfortable with writing that is exploratory, not necessarily assertive, and certainly not authoritative. Many of my favorite posts were written when I didn't understand what I'd read or couldn't make sense of a reading experience. I don't have to work through those limitations before writing a blog post (something I would try to do before writing a review)—I can work through them in a blog post.

Experiment with how you use blogging and how public you make your blogging. You can also consider using a group blog or podcast as a way of engaging in ongoing conversation with colleagues around specific ideas, texts, or evidence. These can be good places to experiment with writing about your scholarly work in language non-specialists can engage with. You can build an audience for your ideas; seek feedback from a wider range of readers, listeners, or viewers; and so on.

All of these modes of communicating your scholarly ideas require specific technical skills, audience-building skills, and developing the ability to write (or communicate) in different genres. Developing those skills may also have other benefits, especially if you are precariously employed in academia. Do not take on this type of communication lightly. Developing these skills takes time. Carefully consider your own goals and have realistic expectations about how others are likely to value the effort you put in and the results you achieve.

Teaching

Teaching may seem like an odd thing to write about in a book about scholarly publishing, but it appears in the acknowledgements sections of too many academic monographs to ignore it as a means of publishing (making public) work in progress. As Aileen Fyfe and colleagues point out in their history of scholarly publishing, the university was initially understood as a community of scholars, and students were understood as active participants in knowledge creation. With the move to mass higher education, increasing class sizes, and formalized qualifications, it can be more difficult to imagine your classroom in this way; but it is an ideal that many academics aspire to, and that may be referred to as research-led or research-informed teaching.

Consider lectures an oral form of scholarly communication in which you synthesize existing scholarly research and offer interpretations. You need to make more of the analytic and interpretive process visible than you would in a conference presentation in order to model scholarship to your students, which offers an opportunity to really work that out. Seminars provide an opportunity to engage more directly with students to test out readings of key texts, get feedback on arguments and approaches, and generate new ideas, while supporting students' development as novice scholars.

Upper-level undergraduate, Master's, and doctoral-level courses offer more opportunities for this type of work. You may even structure an entire course around research, focusing on a particular data set or set of source materials, and taking students through the process of developing research questions, analyzing and interpreting data/sources, and developing arguments. This research may contribute to your more formal publications, acknowledging the role of your students in the research. The students could even collaboratively produce a draft manuscript that you go on to revise and publish with the students as co-authors.

This type of activity is unlikely to be valued in the evaluation of your own research, except insofar as it produces other valuable outputs. It may figure strongly in evaluation of your teaching. It will also reduce the extent to which your teaching competes with your research for your limited time, creating an overlap in which time spent preparing teaching is also time spent moving your research projects forward.

Some questions to consider

For each opportunity of this type, consider the following questions:

How will this type of publishing benefit the development of your ideas, arguments, and research programme? Who would it be beneficial to engage with to this end?

How could publishing your work in this way contribute to your longer-term communication goals?

How could publishing your work in this way help you build networks that will enable you to engage in particular conversations in future?

Does publishing in this way negatively affect your ability to publish this work in more highly valued ways?

Improving Discoverability

As I stated earlier, the primary purpose of academic and scholarly publishing is to communicate with other scholars. To achieve this communicative goal, potential readers need to know that your publication exists and be able to access it. Most academics don't think much about what happens after their manuscripts have been accepted, relying on readers to be thorough in their literature searches and reading practices. To the extent that scholars think about marketing and promotion at all, they think of it as something publishers do for them. I included general comments on the discoverability of different publishing options in the previous chapters, with various reader practices in mind. In this chapter, I propose a more active approach to reaching your readers.

Yes, I am recommending that you promote your own work. The idea of self-promotion is distasteful or just plain nerve-wracking for many scholars. It need not be. This is not about you; it's about your work. You wrote and published that work to make a contribution to knowledge. By letting people know it exists, you are reducing the time and energy they spend looking for relevant scholarship (not to mention their anxiety that they've missed something important), and enabling them to devote more time and energy to developing and publishing their own contributions. As a starting point, I've included sample wording that you can use to promote your work while you get more comfortable with this kind of communication.

Your scholarly readers are busy. Like you, they are juggling research, writing, teaching, administrative roles, committee work, and the many activities of their lives outside of work. Reading may be the most difficult thing to find time for, given its distance from measurable outputs and requirements of enough quiet time and energy to concentrate. Even if you have fairly good reading practices, I suspect you have a long to-read list. Finding time to read things that expand your perspective and seed new ideas is even harder.

I once asked a multidisciplinary group of social science and humanities academics how things got on their to-read list. Everyone in the room was somewhat surprised at the variety of strategies shared. You might try this yourself in a department meeting or an informal gathering of colleagues at a conference. I encourage you to approach this question with curiosity rather than judgement. You might learn about strategies you'd like to try yourself. More importantly, having a better sense of how other scholars discover work can help you improve the discoverability of your own publications.

I have called this chapter "Improving Discoverability" for a reason. Your goal here is to inform people who may be interested that you have published something. You are not requiring anyone to read what you write, much less agree with or praise it. Nor are you convincing them to read it. You are merely pointing out that it exists and is relevant to their work. As difficult as it is, you need to trust that the people who need this knowledge will read it. And remember: it takes a long time for evidence of your impact on the advancement of knowledge to appear.

Titles, keywords, and abstracts

The first step to improving discoverability is to make sure that when people are searching databases your publications turn up in their search. Titles, abstracts, and keywords are not the places to perform your uniqueness. They are the main text that will be searched by scholars looking for relevant material. Thinking carefully about the metadata for your publication and choosing your words carefully with your audience in mind will make a difference. Different search engines will prioritize different kinds of metadata differently, and the main title may very well get preferential treatment. If your publisher makes suggestions about the title, it is very likely based on knowledge of the main databases and how to improve discoverability.

Your title can be creative, but it should also clearly signal the content of your article or book. The title and subtitle should contain important keywords. If you get to list keywords, put yourself in the position of your preferred reader. Key terms that signal your approach or your sources might also go here. Your subject librarian is an expert in categorizing and searching for information. They will be able to help you understand how database searching works so you can make better decisions. They are much more likely to do this for you if you respect their specific expertise, come prepared, and give them a reasonable time frame.

The abstract is both searchable metadata and the primary tool a potential reader will use to decide whether your article needs to be on their to-read list and how high a priority it should have. Everyone is busy. The abstract should in no way resemble clickbait. Spoilers may be unwelcome in popular culture but they are the building blocks of a good abstract. The abstract needs to situate your article in a particular scholarly conversation, clearly indicate your focus or research question, provide relevant information about your methodological and/or theoretical approach, and briefly state your argument. You want them to read the article for the nuance and the detailed evidence, not to find out what your main contribution is. If they cite you based on the abstract alone, make sure that citation will be accurate.

Networking with other scholars

You are part of a network of scholars in your field. This network includes people with whom you have both strong and weak connections. Some you have known for a long time and communicate with frequently. Others are more like scholarly acquaintances. You communicate in person, by phone, by email, and via social media of various types. You will expand your network in various ways. You may meet people in person first, as colleagues or at a conference, and then keep in touch by other means as your careers develop. Or you may meet people initially via email or social media and then in person later (or not at all).

People in your network are interested in knowing what you are up to. Mentors and friends want to know because they care about you as a person. Others will want to know about the project, which they are already aware of in some way. Some people will be waiting for a formal publication that they can cite, put in their course outline/syllabus, or otherwise recommend. Sending an email or other personal communication to let them know that you have a new publication is a nice thing to do. The email does not have to be long. Your subject line could say "FYI, new publication, [title]." The text can remind them of your connection (especially if you don't communicate regularly) and let them know that this publication is now available.

Direct personal communication

There are a few people who you really should communicate with personally, using whatever medium is most appropriate to your relationship. Anyone who helped in any way with the process, whether by encouraging you when you were stuck or publishing work that influenced this piece, would appreciate a brief email. You don't have to contact everyone you cite personally, but it is nice to personally communicate how much you appreciate the work of those who you engage with directly. You don't have to write reams; you can just write, for example, "Thank you for [whatever the contribution was]. My article/book/whatever is now in press [details]." Or (on social media), "Really appreciated the support of [named and tagged person] as I was working on [details of publication, with a link]. Thank you." Or, "The work of [named and tagged person] was really influential as I developed the work now published as [details of publication]."

If you are at a career stage where people are writing references or recommendations for you, it is especially important to let your letter writers know about your publications as soon as they are in press (with the publication date and full bibliographic details). It may even be appropriate to send a copy or ask if they would like you to send a copy: "I appreciate the references/recommendation letters that you write for me. You should know that

I now have another publication in press [details]. Let me know if you'd like me to send you a copy. Thank you."

The purpose of this communication is not to convince the recipient to read the article or book. Nor is it to ask for anything from them. You are merely letting them know it exists because it may be relevant to their interests. The clarity of the subject line helps them triage their email. Providing full details and links to the publisher's website makes it easier for them to access it if they decide they'd like to do so.

Social media

Social media refers to the numerous online platforms that enable you to engage with others: Twitter, Facebook, LinkedIn, and those specifically for academics, like Research Gate and Academia.edu. For my purposes here, it also includes the various email lists that are still in existence. Email lists may feel old-fashioned, but if that is where you engage with other scholars they are relevant to you. In contrast to the previous section, this is the part of your network that it would be inappropriate to send a personal communication. However, the people in these networks share interests, and publication announcements are normal and expected.

Think about what would be appropriate to the specific medium. Check the guidelines for what you can and can't post. On some platforms (e.g. LinkedIn, Research

Gate, etc), the act of adding your new publication to your profile will trigger an alert to anyone who follows you and automatically communicate the new publication to anyone who checks your profile. You could add the details of your most recent publication to your email signature, and to your profile bio on various social media sites.

You can also announce your publication as a status update. Do not do this apologetically. The phrase "shameless self-promotion" is apologetic. It indicates that you think self-promotion really is shameful but you are doing it anyway. Don't waste your character limit. There is nothing wrong with being excited about finishing a project and seeing it out in the world, particularly if you have been talking about the project as you worked on it. Going beyond a mere announcement to convey your excitement about the work itself (not just the fact that it is finally published) will pique other people's interest.

You can even host a virtual book launch on Twitter. Promote it in advance and then post a lot about the book during the specified time, answering questions from (potential) readers. Identify a few interesting things about your book and talk about them, with links to the book. Topics, interesting findings, short quotations, anecdotes about the research process, and so on all make good promotional material. Your goal here is to find hooks that will get people interested enough to click through and read the description and table of contents on the publisher's website. A good hashtag will help bring people into your event. Twitter stories can be used to good effect for this purpose, too. Your publisher may be willing to help out with this.

If you use Facebook for professional networking, you could use Facebook Live to talk about the book and answer questions. You could also set up a Facebook page for the book or a Facebook group to host discussions about your book. You could do this during the writing phase and then host a virtual launch party in your group when it comes out. Or, set one up once you've got the publishing date. The pay-to-play model Facebook uses for pages (and, increasingly, groups) limits your reach, but it can be a good virtual location to collect people already in your network.

Make sure to share links to blog posts, reviews, and other writing about your book on your own social media channels. Reach out to relevant podcasts and blogs for reviews or to propose an interview, and then promote them before and after broadcast/publication.

Reciprocity is crucial to effective social media engagement. Share other people's publication announcements. Post about what you are reading and what you like about it. Attend virtual books launches. You don't need to do a lot but being on social media regularly will both build an audience and make your promotional material more effective.

Conferences, seminars, blogs, etc.

We commonly think of conferences, seminars, blogs and so on as venues to disseminate scholarly work, and this is how I have treated them in the earlier chapters of this *Short Guide*. However, they are also venues for promoting your formal publications in various ways.

Large conferences with a publishers' book fair offer opportunities for you to work with your publisher to organize a book-launch event for your monograph or edited collection. This could be as simple as a reception with a brief presentation by you about the book, followed by informal discussions. Do not wait for your publisher to propose this (see the next section). You could go further and organize a conference panel around the book, either presenting some of the material in it (especially if it is an edited collection) or inviting scholars to present papers taking the work in new directions. If your book is particularly suited to being used in teaching, you could make that the focus of the panel (instead of the more usual research findings), perhaps inviting colleagues to speak specifically to pedagogy, or working with others whose recent books complement your own.

Conferences can also be used to raise awareness of journal articles. Although conference presentations often focus on works in progress that will later be published as journal articles, things do not need to go in this order. You may be able to present work already accepted for publication. This is particularly appropriate if you did not present the work in progress to this particular audience. Of course, if you did present the work in progress prior to publication, there are probably already people interested in knowing about the publication. Remember to mention (in appropriate ways) that your paper is now published when you are catching up with colleagues in the informal spaces of the conference.

Invited seminars and blog posts (on your own blog or as guest posts on other blogs) are a very good way to promote new publications, especially if you publish books. Create your own book tour by combining a seminar with a local book launch to encourage attendance, provide opportunities to discuss the work, and perhaps even sell copies (using the local bookstore). Virtual book tours (guest posts and interviews on relevant blogs) allow you to extend your reach beyond the limitations of geography and the time and energy you have available to travel.

Preprints (in fields that have them) and early electronic publication of journal articles that will later be published in print are also good ways to build a readership for the final publication. Use social media to share the link. Or write a blog post focusing on one aspect of the work, with a link to the preprint. Don't forget to also announce the formal print publication when it is available.

Getting the most out of your publisher

The publisher of your scholarly work also has an interest in your work being read and cited. You are more knowledgeable about the content of your book or article than anyone working at the publishing house, and the marketing people will rely on you to provide the information they need to do their part well. Book publishers usually provide you with a long marketing form with a series of questions. Take this very seriously. It is always worth asking your editor (of the journal or books series, or the acquisitions editor of the press) what support they can provide and what their basic level of marketing is. Your editor or a member of the marketing staff may be willing to help you learn the particular styles of writing necessary for good marketing material.

The publisher is generally responsible for ensuring that publications are indexed and abstracted in relevant databases. They will have digital and print catalogues of their books. They will likely spend some of their marketing budget on stalls in the publishers' fairs of conferences relevant to their whole list. The primary reason publishers attend conferences is to prospect for new material they can publish, but they also use them to promote recent publications.

Publishers also provide review copies to scholarly journals that have book-review sections. This is particularly important for improving the discoverability of books because journals are more easily searchable. A book review can be found in a database search (including citations searches, since the reference to your book in the review is a citation) and will lead readers to your book. It is your responsibility to let the publisher know which journals would be appropriate.

Your publisher may be willing to provide books, and possibly funding, for a book launch, readings, or other events to publicize your book (or special issue of a journal). They are unlikely to organize these things independently. Approach your editor to discuss a small reception or other book-launch event at relevant conferences, especially those you know the press will be attending. They should also nominate you for any prizes for which your book is eligible, and will welcome information from you about such prizes.

For local events or conferences your publisher is not attending, it is probably more appropriate to work with a local bookseller, which can order books and have a sales table at the event. Bookstores typically acquire stock on a "sale or return" basis, which means they are not stuck with books they can't sell. A local bookseller that does a reasonable amount of academic business (e.g. course texts) may also be willing to host an event on their premises. Your publisher may provide flyers, bookmarks, or other printed promotional material that you can distribute at in-person events.

If your book would be appropriate as a course text, you will have indicated that on the publisher's marketing questionnaire. Complement the publisher's general marketing of course texts by contacting colleagues who you know teach appropriate courses to let them know your book is out. You do not need to convince them to use it. You are merely letting them know it is now available. If inspection copies are available from the publisher, let them know that. If you are willing to answer questions about whether the book will meet their specific pedagogical needs, say so explicitly. Don't offer to do anything you don't want to do.

You may receive free copies of your book. The numbers are usually limited. Check the rules for your promotion portfolio before giving away all the free copies, in case you need to save these copies for external evaluators. You might also use them to thank anyone who helped you significantly as you worked on the project. If it's a book that came from your dissertation, your supervisor or external examiner might appreciate a copy. You could also prioritize those who might be interested but don't typically read academic books or have access to academic libraries.

It isn't just book publishers that provide support for promotion. Journal publishers also provide authors with a limited number of free copies of the article, to distribute as the author wishes. In the past, these were offprints, and extra copies needed to be ordered in advance. These days, they are provided as free electronic download codes. It is worth thinking about how you use these free copies to solidify your scholarly network and build relationships with journalists, policy makers, and others who may find your work interesting or useful. You don't have to use them right away; there may be benefit to saving some codes for future use.

When you contact people in your network to tell them about your new publication, you can include the code for a free copy, or let them know you have free copies available if they do not have access to the journal through their own library. Keep some for journalists who write on related topics, especially if you already have a relationship. Let your media and communications office know they are available even if you contact journalists directly. Letting your social media followers know you have free copies if they need them, and asking them to contact you for the code, can be a way to solidify an online relationship—and is less awkward than offering a copy to a specific individual who you don't know well but suspect might be interested.

Some questions to consider

> List members of your scholarly network who would be interested in knowing how your career is progressing. Highlight those who write references for you or provide other direct support for your career.

List members of your scholarly network who would be interested in how your research is progressing.

The above two lists probably overlap a bit, but combined they comprise your scholarly network. Make some notes about the most appropriate means of communicating with them (personal/general), whether they need a copy of the publication, etc.

Are there conferences coming up in the next year that potential readers of your publication will be attending? Brainstorm possibilities for announcing or promoting your publication. Add criteria related to expanding the readership of your publication to your list of decision criteria for prioritizing which conferences you will attend.

Are you active on social media, an email list, or a blog? Brainstorm possibilities for announcing and/or promoting your publication on each platform you are already active on.

Is this publication the kind of thing you might be invited to speak to a departmental or research group seminar series about? If so, do you have colleagues who could invite you to speak in a series they are involved in, or who could recommend you to whoever is organizing their local speaker series?

If you are publishing a book (monograph or edited collection), think about a book launch (or more than one). Where might a reasonable number of potential readers be able to gather? Do you want a face-to-face event, a virtual launch, or both? Who might help organize?

If you are publishing a book, reviews are an important way to improve discoverability—both through database searches that pick up journal content and through web searches. Have you provided your publisher with a list of appropriate journals that publish reviews and reach the target readership for your book? Do you know anyone who could review your book (for a journal or on their blog)? Have you approached them to suggest that they review it?

Notes and Further Reading

What is Publishing and Why Do It?

The quotation from Margaret Atwood is from her speech "The Publishing Pie" (February 15, 2011, youtu.be/-6iMBf6Ddjk).

The quotation from Aileen Fyfe and colleagues can be found on page 4 of *Untangling Academic Publishing: A history of the relationship between commercial interests, academic prestige and the circulation of research* (2017, doi.org/10.5281/zenodo.546100, open access). The authors cite HESA (2016), Blackmore (2016), and Blackmore & Kandiko (2011) in support of their claims in this quotation (full references in their paper, which is open access.) I recommend this report for a brief history of the relationship between scholarly publications, prestige, and academic careers with a focus on the UK context.

I use the generic term "validation processes" throughout this *Short Guide* because the process will vary depending on where you are and your stage of career. Validation processes are those processes that use your publication record to evaluate the quality of your scholarly work and include hiring, promotion, tenure review, confirmation of permanent employment, funding competitions, awards competitions, institutional accreditation processes, the Research Excellence Framework (REF) (in the UK), and so on.

For an example of how the validation narrative dominates discussions of scholarly publishing, see Sharon McCulloch, "The Importance of Being REF-able", in which she reports on research on academic writers and the impact of managerial cultures on academic writing and identity (February 9, 2017, *LSE Impact blog*, blogs.lse.ac.uk/impactofsocialsciences/2017/02/09/the-importance-of-being-ref-able-academic-writing-under-pressure-from-a-culture-of-counting/).

Different validation processes may use different terms for the impact on the advancement of knowledge, including "impact", "significance", and "contribution". Whatever specific meanings these terms take on in various validation processes, the principles I outline here are common to all academic contexts. For example, in the UK REF, the term "significance" is used to mean the significance of the impact on the advancement of scholarly knowledge and the term "impact" to more narrowly refer to impact on the knowledge of those beyond the academy.

I have taken the conceptual framework of instrumental, conceptual, and symbolic use from Nabil Amara, Mathieu Ouimet, & Réjean Landry (2004), "New Evidence on Instrumental, Conceptual, and Symbolic Utilization of University Research in Government Agencies", *Science Communication*, Vol 26, No 1, pp. 75–106. They developed this framework to understand how research gets used in government policymaking. I have extended their conceptual framework to consider all uses of scholarly research, including by other scholars.

Audience, Form, Outlet

The opening quotation is from Kenneth Burke, *The Philosophy of Literary Form* (University of California Press, 1941, pp. 110–11).

Charlotte Mathieson (who is in the humanities) has written about her experience of publishing her dissertation as a book, and more generally about publishing for early-career researchers:

- "How to get published as an #ECR" (March 3, 2016, StylishAcademic.com/getting-published-ecr).
- "Publishing strategies as an ECR" (July 6, 2016, CharlotteMathieson.wordpress.com/2016/07/06/publishing-strategies-as-an-ecr-phd-publishing-workshop-5th-july-2016/).

There is also a good set of links to resources on publishing your dissertation on *Hook & Eye*: "From dissertation to book: Academic book publishing resources" (March

30, 2017) HookandEye.ca/2017/03/30/from-dissertation-to-book-academic-book-publishing-resources/

The quotation from Aileen Fyfe and colleagues can be found on page 4 of Aileen Fyfe et al. (2017), *Untangling Academic Publishing* DOI 10.5281/zenodo.546100.

The following are good starting points for those wanting to learn more about open-access scholarly publishing.

- Peter Suber has published "A very brief introduction to open access" (legacy.earlham.edu/~peters/fos/brief.htm) and a brief "Open access overview" (legacy.earlham.edu/~peters/fos/overview.htm). Both contain lots of references to follow up.
- Suber has also written a book: *Open Access* (MIT Press, 2012). Details, updates, and reviews are available here: bit.ly/oa-book
- Specifically in relation to the humanities, see Martin Eve, *Open Access & the Humanities* (Cambridge University Press, 2014), DOI 10.1017/CBO9781316161012 (this book itself is open access).

Open access is not a magic wand. You still need to think about discoverability. The complexities of the issues are a frequent topic of discussion at *The Scholarly Kitchen* (ScholarlyKitchen.sspnet.org). See, for example, Anne Powell's guest post, "Availability does not equal access" (May 21, 2015):

ScholarlyKitchen.sspnet.org/2015/05/21/guest-post-inasps-anne-powell-on-availability-does-not-equal-access/

Intellectual property rights are complicated. The most important one you need to consider is copyright. Many publishers will ask you to assign copyright to them, reserving your moral right to be acknowledged as the author and so on, though you may have an option to license specific rights to them. Their standard agreements for licensing may amount to the same thing. Your ability to deposit a copy in a preprint archive or institutional repository will be affected by these arrangements. If you are publishing an early version of something that may later become a chapter in monograph, this will also be affected by the copyright arrangements. Unfortunately, I do not have a quick and easy guide to copyright for academics. If your funder or institution requires open-access publishing in some form (including depositing in an institutional repository), they will have legal advice available to you. It will be primarily to protect the institution's position but is still worth listening to. Your scholarly association may also have advice for members. You may be eligible to join the Society of Authors, or equivalent organization for authors in your country, which will entitle you to legal advice about copyright and related issues. If there is something specific that you want to be able to do with a particular piece of writing, ask the publisher explicitly whether that will be allowed and whether the licensing agreement can make it possible. Then get someone with legal expertise to check that the terms of the contract do actually allow it. Keep any written (including email) correspondence in which they (the publisher and anyone else) assure you that it is, just in case.

Some of the questions at the end of this chapter also appear in Chapter 3 ("From process to product: Who are you writing for?") of *The Scholarly Writing Process*. The quotation from Dorothy E. Smith can be found on page 46 of her *The Everyday World as Problematic: a feminist sociology* (Open University Press, 1988). The passage in which it is found was also quoted in Chapter 3 of *The Scholarly Writing Process*, which also gives a bit more context.

Books

One high-profile challenge to the dominance of the monograph in validation processes has come from a task force of the Modern Language Association of America. In 2007, the Association published *Report of the MLA Task Force on Evaluating Scholarship for Tenure and Promotion*, which included the recommendation:

> The profession as a whole should develop a more capacious conception of scholarship by rethinking the dominance of the monograph, promoting the scholarly essay, establishing multiple pathways to tenure, and using scholarly portfolios.

The association has gone on to produce guidelines and statements for various types of publication found to be undervalued, including scholarly editions, translations, digital humanities, digital media, and electronic journals. (A list can be found under the heading "Publishing and Scholarship" on the "Surveys, Reports, and Other Documents" page of the MLA website.)

It is possible to use a single pen name for the authorial voice of co-authors of a monograph. For example, J.K. Gibson-Graham (a collaboration between Julie Graham and Katherine Gibson) published several articles and books, beginning with *The End of Capitalism (As We Knew It)* (Blackwell, 1996; 2nd ed 2006). The Wikipedia page about this author is informative: en.wikipedia.org/wiki/J._K._Gibson-Graham

An example of using edited collections to bring scholarly work to a popular audience are several volumes, published by Wiley, that bring together serious historical scholarship with popular cultural themes: *Harry Potter & History* (2011), *Star Wars and History* (2012), *The Hobbit and History* (2014), *Game of Thrones vs History* (2017). See also The Blackwell Philosophy and Pop Culture Series, also published by Wiley.

I have written about one of my own early publications as an example of considering an invitation to contribute to a special issue or edited collection in relation to your communicative goals: "Who do you want to reach: An example" (May 17, 2010) JoVanEvery.ca/who-do-you-want-to-reach-example

Thanks to Rohan Maitzen for helping me clarify the definition of the critical or scholarly edition. See also MLA's *Guidelines for Editors of Scholarly Editions* (2011). On changes to the scholarly edition due to technological advances, see MLA's *Statement on the Scholarly Edition in the Digital Age* (2017). Available from the MLA website.

My warning that you may need to explain the nature of the scholarly edition to colleagues on multidisciplinary review committees is based on Michele Lamont's finding, in her study of interdisciplinary grant panels, that one of the customary rules of deliberation is "deferring to expertise and observing disciplinary sovereignty." See Chapter 4 of her *How Professors Think* (Harvard University Press, 2009)

If you've decided that a book is what you want to write, William Germano's books on how to write serious nonfiction come highly recommended:

- *Getting It Published: A guide for scholars and anyone else serious about serious books* (University of Chicago Press, 3rd ed 2016) is for anyone writing a new book (not revising a dissertation).
- *From Dissertation to Book* (University of Chicago Press, 2nd ed 2013) is for those who are revising a dissertation into a book (or need more information about that process to decide whether to do so).

If you are considering writing a trade book based on your research, see Susan Rabiner & Alfred Fortunato, *Thinking Like Your Editor: How to write great serious nonfiction and get it published* (W.W. Norton, 2003).

In the section on choosing a publisher, I have chosen not to discuss self-publishing. With the exception of blogs, podcasts, and video (as complements to more formal publishing), self-publishing is likely to remain a poor relation to the more well-established outlets in both validation processes and the decision-making processes of scholars deciding what work to prioritize in the limited time they have to keep up with the literature in their field. Helen Kara and Nathan Ryder have written specifically on the topic of self-publishing for academics: *Self-Publishing for Academics* (2016, Know More Publishing).

The Alliance of Independent Authors publishes a guide to self-publishing services, which also includes useful information for distinguishing between small independent publishers and such services: Jim Giammatteo & John Doppler, *Choosing the Best Self-Publishing Companies and Services 2018: How to self-publish your book (Alliance of Independent Authors' Self-Publishing Success Series)* (Alliance of Independent Authors, 2018, updated annually)

On negotiating with publishers, Helen Kara has written "Why and how to negotiate with academic book publishers" (6 March, 2018) HelenKara.com/2018/03/06/why-and-how-to-negotiate-with-academic-book-publishers/. She focuses on royalty rates, but the same principles can also be applied to negotiating about other things, like copyright.

I strongly recommend that you use a professional indexer to produce your index. If your publisher is arranging the index, ask if they are using a professional. Indexers have their own professional associations where you can find someone with expertise in your area. (See e.g. the UK Society of Indexers) Indexing is a specialist skill. No matter how well you know the material, developing the skill of indexing while producing your own index is not a good use of your limited time. Nor is it a good use of research assistants' time. Furthermore, producing a useful index involves much more than using software to search for specified terms in the text and collate the page numbers. Helen Kara has a good post about the importance of the index to non-fiction books: "Let's talk about the index" (April 10, 2018): HelenKara.com/2018/04/10/lets-talk-about-the-index/. To learn more about indexing and what it involves, Sylvia Coates has created a free course, "Indexing books as a career", which is also suitable for authors and editors: www.SylviaCoates.com/indexing-books-as-a-career-free-mooc.html

When considering when to secure a publishing contract, the four tendencies (Upholders, Questioners, Obligers, and Rebels) described by Gretchin Rubin in her book about habits, *Better than Before* (Two Roads, 2016), provide a useful heuristic for thinking about how you respond to deadlines and other forms of external pressure.

Peer-Reviewed Journals

I have written about one of my own early publications as an example of considering an invitation to contribute to a special issue or edited collection in relation to your communicative goals: "Who do you want to reach: An example" (May 17, 2010) JoVanEvery.ca/who-do-you-want-to-reach-example

The discussion of the peer-reviewed journal as a discourse community in Chapter 2 of Pat Thomson and Barbara Kamler, *Writing for Peer Reviewed Journals* (Routledge, 2013) is a more detailed look at this idea that your publication is contributing to an ongoing conversation with a particular focus on how a particular journal situates itself in relation to particular scholarly conversations. *They Say/I Say* by Gerald Graff and Cathy Birkenstein (W.W. Norton, 4th ed 2018) comes highly recommended as a resource for working out how to situate your own argument in relation to a discourse community.

"Self-plagiarism" is a contested term. Check the journal's or publisher's policies prior to submission. Your institution or scholarly association will include information on self-plagiarism in their research integrity policies.

On self-plagiarism, Sarah Elaine Eaton & Katherine Crossman's (2018) "Self-Plagiarism Research Literature in the Social Sciences: A scoping review" (*Interchange*, Vol 49, No 285, DOI 10.1007/s10780-018-9333-6) aims to provide a comprehensive review of the literature on self-plagiarism and is thus a good starting point for further reading. They note that very little of the literature is based on primary, or even secondary, research but rather dominated by editorials and editorial responses.

Jamie L. Callahan (2017) makes an argument against the use of the term "self-plagiarism" in "The Retrospective (Im)moralization of Self-Plagiarism: Power interests in the social construction of new norms for publishing" (*Organization*, Vol 25, No 3, pp. 305–19, DOI 10.1177/1350508417734926). She defends some of the activities that sometimes fall under its umbrella in terms very similar to what I argue in this *Short Guide* about audience, publishing several outputs from a single research project, and the evolution of a publication through various forms of what I call "work-in-progress publishing".

Learning how to cite your own work appropriately is a bit tricky, as becomes clear in the section on self-citation as a hedge against self-plagiarism in the Callahan article. Pat Thomson has a useful series of blog posts covering the main issues:

- "Citing yourself—how much is too much?" (May 8, 2017, PatThomson.net/2017/05/08/citing-yourself-how-much-is-too-much/) provides a good overview of the main concerns regarding when it is appropriate.
- "Citing yourself—in the text" (May 11, 2017, PatThomson.net/2017/05/11/citing-yourself-in-the-text/) covers the mechanics.
- "On the perils of self-citation" (August 24, 2015, PatThomson.net/2015/08/24/on-the-perils-of-self-citation/) gives some good examples of the kind of thing you want to avoid.

Librarians and scholarly associations are producing guides to assist scholars in identifying predatory journals and conferences. See, for example, Sarah Eaton, *Avoiding Predatory Journals and Questionable Conferences: A resource guide* (University of Calgary, 2018), DOI 10.5072/PRISM/20

Publishing Work in Progress

On the ways online forms of publishing may be tainted by their similarity to oral communication, see Bonnie Stewart "Academic Twitter & academic capital: Collapsing orality & literacy in scholarly publics", in Deborah Lupton, Inger Mewburn & Pat Thomson (Eds), *The Digital Academic: Critical perspectives of digital technologies in higher education* (Routledge, 2018). Stewart's argument in this chapter has also influenced the way I talk about the status of different types of outputs throughout this *Short Guide*.

In her discussion of self-plagiarism, Pat Thomson (2011) raises the issue of whether a paper that is substantially the same as one presented at a conference and archived in a repository is "unpublished" (PatThomson.net/2011/11/12/self-plagiarism-and-online-publication...-some-musings/). As scholarly publishing changes in response to technological innovation, these issues are somewhat unsettled. See the list of further reading on this topic in the notes to the previous chapter. At the very least, you should always acknowledge earlier or related versions of a paper when submitting.

One should not assume that working papers did not circulate widely prior to the digital age. For example, the Centre for Contemporary Cultural Studies at the University of Birmingham had a very popular series of working papers, which were still circulating as photocopies 20 years after the Centre itself had closed and many of its members had moved on to work in other institutions. When I was working in the department that succeeded the Centre in the late 1990s, the departmental secretary regularly received requests by email or post, photocopied working papers, and posted them out.

The quotation from Rohan Maitzen about blogging can be found on her blog in the post "Definitely not a review of Mary McCarthy's The Group" (March 19, 2018): RohanMaitzen.com/2018/03/19/definitely-not-a-review-of-mary-mccarthys-the-group/ For more on using blogs and social media to communicate your scholarship, see Cat Pausé & Deborah Russell (2016), "Sociable scholarship: The use of social media in the 21st century academy", *Journal of Applied Social Theory*, Vol 1, No 1.

A brief history of the changing role of universities, including the relationship between professors and students, can be found in Aileen Fyfe et al. (2017), *Untangling Academic Publishing* DOI 10.5281/zenodo.546100

One example of collaborating with students on research that leads to publication is Michelle Moravec's work. She teaches at a small liberal arts college in Pennsylvania. Student research was central to the following article (and is acknowledged in a footnote): Michelle Moravec (2016), "'Till I've Done All That I Can'": An Auxiliary Nurse's Memories of World War I", *Historical Reflexions/Réflexions Historique*, Vol 42, No 3, pp. 71–90 DOI 10.3167/hrrh.2016.420305. Moravec has also published with students as co-authors: Michelle Moravec, Elizabeth Bolton, Kyah Hawkins, Sabrina Heggan, Jeel Rao & Hope Smalley (2017), "The Great War through Women's Eyes", *Pennsylvania History*, Vol 84, No 4, pp. 452–61 (Project MUSE: muse.jhu.edu/article/672912).

Improving Discoverability

On writing abstracts, I recommend Pat Thomson and Barbara Kamler, *Writing for Peer Reviewed Journals* (Routledge, 2013), which provides a clear model, with variations, situating it in the authors' discussion of journals as discourse communities. They propose writing an abstract, which they refer to as a "tiny text", early in the process to clarify your own thinking and use as a guide to the writing. You may need to rewrite the abstract before submission. Raul Pacheco-Vega has also collected several resources about writing abstracts in his blog post "How to write an abstract for a paper" (July 18, 2018): www.raulpacheco.org/2018/07/how-to-write-an-abstract-for-a-paper/

I am grateful to everyone who responded to Tina Adcock's request for ideas about how to promote a book on social media: twitter.com/i/moments/996203100292636672

Before presenting already-published work at a conference, check the conference guidelines. If there is no claim to first refusal for publications and you are honest about the status of your paper, it should not be a problem. Also see the notes on conference papers and self-plagiarism in the previous chapter.

Helen Kara has a good post about marketing academic books: "How to market your academic book" (November 7, 2017): HelenKara.com/2017/11/07/how-to-market-your-academic-book/

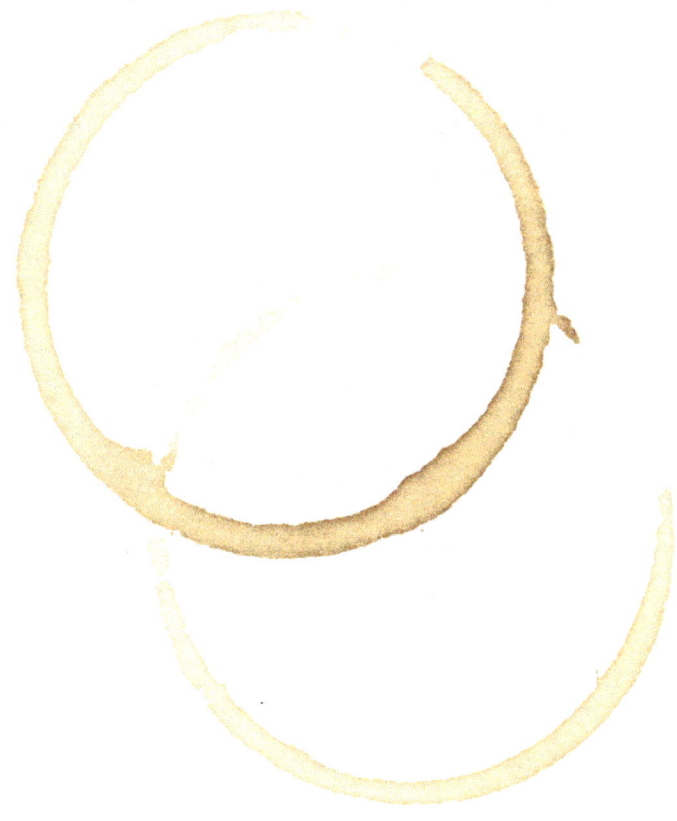

Acknowledgements

Some say that we write what we need to hear. I wish someone had explained some of the things in this *Short Guide* to me more clearly when I was starting my academic career. Advice about *how* to publish a book was much more easily available than advice about *why* to do so. I have often wondered if some of my work might have had more impact on particular debates had I published differently.

I gained considerable insight into the *why* of scholarly publishing from my work as both a programme officer and policy analyst for the Social Sciences and Humanities Research Council of Canada. The opportunity to meet Michelle Lamont while she was working on her study of peer review was particularly appreciated. It was also during this time that I came across the work of Réjean Landry on research use, which I have pondered for many years since. I'm sure there are many other people and conversations from that period that have influenced my thinking. Thank you to everyone I worked with during those years.

As I said in *The Scholarly Writing Process*, the first *Short Guide* in this series, we often develop our ideas through writing. Much of what is contained here was first elaborated for my blog: JoVanEvery.ca. I have also benefited from conversations with many of those in my Twitter network.

I would like to thank several people for helping me understand specific types of publications (any errors or misrepresentations are my own). Frances Wooley provided details about working papers. Rohan Maitzen helped me understand the scholarly edition. Martin Eve provided references about open-access publishing. Catherine Anderson helped clarify some points about open-source textbooks. Michelle Moravec clarified some points about writing and publishing with students. Janice Liedl spoke frequently of her involvement in various books on history and popular culture, published by the Wiley series on history and popular culture (some of which she has contributed to and/or edited).

Katherine Firth helped me clarify what I meant by "reader," and both she and Helen Kara helped me figure out how to approach the issue of self-plagiarism. Raul Pacheco-Vega's reading notes on books about writing books heavily influenced the further reading suggestions. Thank you to everyone I chat to on Twitter about these and related issues.

I highly recommend working with an editor. Hannah Austin edited the manuscript and made some excellent substantive changes that resulted in a better book. Amy Crook designed the cover and the interior of the print edition. Thank you to the Alliance of Independent Authors for the wealth of practical advice they provide on self-publishing. Now that I'm on my fourth self-published book, I'm starting to feel like I know what I'm doing. I take full responsibility for all the decisions I have made based on the excellent advice of these professionals.

About the Author

Jo VanEvery transforms academic lives from surviving to thriving. She used to be an academic sociologist and then a programme officer for a funding agency. Now she helps you juggle your myriad responsibilities, provides a structure so you can get more writing done, helps you clarify your vision and make a plan for the next part of the path towards it, and boosts your confidence so you can do the work that makes your heart sing. You can read more of her writing on her website, JoVanEvery.ca; follow her on Twitter, Twitter.com/JoVanEvery; or like her Facebook page, Facebook.com/JoVEAcademicCareerCoach/.

Also by Jo VanEvery

Finding Time For Your Scholarly Writing: A Short Guide (2018) ISBN 978-1-912040-70-4 (pb) 978-1-912040-69-8 (e-book)

The Principles of Juggling: A Picture Book for Academics (2017) ISBN 978-1-912040-71-1 (pb)

The Scholarly Writing Process: A Short Guide (2016) ISBN 978-1-912040-64-3 (pb) 978-1-912040-72-8 (e-book)

Coming soon

I have several more *Short Guides* in various stages of preparation on topics including peer review, saying no, and optimizing focus. To hear about new publications in the series, get excerpts, and hear about work in progress, subscribe to my newsletter: JoVanEvery.ca/newsletters/

www.ingramcontent.com/pod-product-compliance
Lightning Source LLC
Chambersburg PA
CBHW071350080526
44587CB00017B/3037